To: Pat + Donna Mat

The two of you are such a blessing to me, my family and the Body of Christ. Continue to let the love and light of Christ shine through you in all you say + do. Your quiet strength and deep love for God inspires me greatly! Praying that you will follow your dreams and walk in the fullness of all the God has for you and your family.

Abundant Blessings,
Christina

Mark 9:23

November 2012

Standing on the Promises

Discover the Power of Unshakable Faith

Christina M. Whitaker

Copyright © 2012 Christina M. Whitaker

All rights reserved. No part of this book may be used or reproduced by any means, graphic, electronic, or mechanical, including photocopying, recording, taping or by any information storage retrieval system without the written permission of the publisher except in the case of brief quotations embodied in critical articles and reviews.

WestBow Press books may be ordered through booksellers or by contacting:

WestBow Press
A Division of Thomas Nelson
1663 Liberty Drive
Bloomington, IN 47403
www.westbowpress.com
1-(866) 928-1240

Because of the dynamic nature of the Internet, any web addresses or links contained in this book may have changed since publication and may no longer be valid. The views expressed in this work are solely those of the author and do not necessarily reflect the views of the publisher, and the publisher hereby disclaims any responsibility for them.

Any people depicted in stock imagery provided by Thinkstock are models, and such images are being used for illustrative purposes only.

Certain stock imagery © Thinkstock.

ISBN: 978-1-4497-6683-2 (sc)
ISBN: 978-1-4497-6684-9 (e)
ISBN: 978-1-4497-6685-6 (hc)

Library of Congress Control Number: 2012916744

Printed in the United States of America

WestBow Press rev. date: 09/26/2012

Table Of Contents

Introduction 4
Chapter 1: Reflections 9
Chapter 2: Strike One 15
Chapter 3: Strike Two 21
Chapter 4: Strike Three 27
Chapter 5: Simply Amazing 37
Chapter 6: Created to Stand 47
Chapter 7: I Will Not Die 59
Chapter 8: Focus Forward 67
Chapter 9: Delight in Him 79
Chapter 10: Be Ready When Opportunity Knocks 85
Chapter 11: The Fight of Your Life 91
Chapter 12: Reality Strikes 103
Chapter 13: Obedience 111
Chapter 14: Learning to Rest in Him 119
Chapter 15: Honor Releases Breakthrough 127
Chapter 16: The Road to Unshakable Faith 135
Chapter 17: Don't Give Up 145
Chapter 18: Finding the Pavilion of God 151
Chapter 19: Your Waiting is not in Vain 157
Chapter 20: Another Dimension of Blessing 163
Chapter 21: Birthing Your Promise 171
Epilogue 179

ACKNOWLEDGEMENTS

To my children, Olivia and Gabrielle, thank you for your patience, I love you more than words can say. To my parents, I am forever grateful for the rich investments of love and wisdom that you so generously made in my life. To Pastor Adrian and Shandi Starks, I do not have the words to adequately express my sincere appreciation for all that you have done for me and my family, over the past ten years. To Taiwan Brown, my prayer partner and closest friend, a million thanks for your mentorship, partnership and your willingness to pray without ceasing in the midnight hour. To my husband Antonio, the love of my life, thank you for teaching me the true meaning of unshakable faith.

In diligent pursuit...

Introduction

I stood on top of the mountain. The blustery wind howled around me. After hours of climbing, with frequent pauses to gather my strength and my nerve, I made it to the top. Jagged rocks along the way dug into my hands leaving trails of dried blood. The joy in my heart far outweighed the pain in my hands. I made it. I stood atop a height I never thought I would reach. A surge of pride mixed with utter exhaustion filled my chest. Relief washed over me. What a surreal moment. I had scaled the mountain successfully.

I waited in a narrow room at the top of the mountain. Around me people were strapping on colorful parachutes and leaping off the mountainside. Two female guides congratulated me on reaching the top of the legendary mountain. Again, great pride filled my chest and warmed my heart, as though I had just downed a cup of java. The congratulatory moment faded as the two women issued final instructions on jumping off the mountain. They were stern but helpful. They reviewed with me the lengthy list of do's and don'ts.

I rested briefly on a wooden bench and listened intently to further instructions. My questions were few, though my fear was enormous. Only a couple of people stood before me in line. The euphoria of this great accomplishment was short-lived, because my journey was not yet complete. My moment of truth drew closer. It would soon be my turn to leap off the mountain. One would think ascending a great mountain was enough, but I knew that leaping off the mountain was something I must do as well.

My hands shook with a mix of adrenaline, anticipation and fear. I pressed my hands into my pockets to mask the nervous shaking and coax them to settle down. Successfully ascending a mountain was one thing, but leaping off it with nothing more than an airy parachute, was quite another. My mouth grew desperately dry, stomach churned, heart raced and my once sturdy knees started to buckle. The moment of truth knocked at my door and I debated whether to open the door that loomed before me.

All too quickly, it was my turn. I took several deep breaths and gathered my composure. I mustered some faith and stepped out onto the platform. I stood atop a narrow wooden platform, overlooking the coast of Nepal. The view was breathtaking and terribly intimidating. I could see distant pieces of many nations from where I was perched. Was I really about to jump off this legendary mountain?

My time had come. All eyes turned to me. It was now or never. With my parachute securely fastened I walked to the edge of the platform and tried to keep my nervous shaking to a minimum. I gathered my nerve, whispered a desperate prayer for safety, and I pulled the rip cord. The parachute deployed and opened inside the narrow room at the top of the mountain! My feet were still planted on the platform. I had failed to jump!

The parachute ballooned open filling the small room. It created quite a chaotic scene. Several people came to my rescue stripping the deployed chute from my fearful frame.

The guides flailed their arms and shouted, "No, no. You must jump first, and then pull the cord!"

As a result of my first falter, all eyes now rested on me. The guides gave me a new parachute and helped me secure it. Sweat streamed down my brow. I was more frightened than ever, but I was also more determined than ever. I knew I would do it. This was my time. I had not come this far to turn back. I gathered my nerve, took a few deep breaths, got a running start and leaped out into the air, off the snow covered mountain.

The wind was brutally cold on my face and would have stung my eyes if not for the protective goggles. I closed my eyes and took several deep breaths. I recall feeling great peace as I soared thru the air much like an eagle. A yellow sky diver's suit protected my small frame from the blustery wind. Fear and concern evaporated as the currents of wind carried me through the sky. Cares and worries, which usually weighed so heavily upon me, seemed a million miles away. The wind was so strong and supportive. It seemed to carry me with the greatest of care. And at the right time, I did pull the ripcord as the guides had demonstrated.

Many peaceful moments after I deployed the parachute, I opened my eyes and looked up. To my absolute horror, I saw that my parachute was slightly tangled, and the ground was quickly approaching. I stretched with all my might, against the force of the wind, and reached my hand up as best I could, and gave the parachute strings several hard tugs and vigorous shakes. I did not have time to become frantic. I knew time was of the essence and panic would only make things worse. I moved the parachute strings a few more times and it untangled and expanded. Seconds later, I landed on the ground in a place I'd never seen before. It was a new place.

Mission complete! I jumped off the mountain and landed successfully. Utter relief flooded my soul. I crumpled to the ground, overwhelmed with exhaustion. I took a moment to rest, lying amidst my parachute like a sleeping child. I heard a siren approaching. The sound grew louder and louder. The siren blared, coming closer and closer. The siren was so loud. Suddenly, I sat straight up and slammed my hand down on my alarm clock. I was drenched in sweat and breathing heavily. The siren was only my alarm clock, not an approaching rescue vehicle. It had all been an incredible dream!

My mind raced as I recounted the dream that seemed to be engrained in my memory. It seemed so real, the wind in my face, the height of the mountain, the jagged press of the rocks in my hands and even the dive off the side of the mountain. It would be a few years before I understood the meaning of this puzzle in the night. One thing was certain, a great leap of faith was coming. A leap of faith that would require me to stretch beyond anything I have yet known.

Whether you realize it or not, God has a plan for your life, and each day you have opportunity to take steps in the direction of your destiny, or further away from it. Even when you do not know the thoughts or plans God has for you, He does. Even when you cannot see your expected end, He can. God is in the midst of your life, and He is ever working toward bringing you to your expected end.

If you are one who has ever felt like giving up, this book was written with you in mind. Written in faith, to ignite your faith, and remind you that God has not forgotten about you. All that He has promised you is sure. This book will help enlighten and guide you to a place of apprehending the promises of God. You will learn how to plant your feet firmly on the promises of God and stand in faith without succumbing to the storms of life. This book will give you practical keys for navigating life's peaks, valleys and the many places in-between. No matter what you have faced thus far, there is a plan of success and victory for your life.

God charted the course of your destiny before you were ever conceived. God knows your end from the beginning and every pit stop in-between. There is a providential plan and purpose for your life. Even if you have drifted from your course, there is hope and promise for you. It is the will of God for you to walk out His perfect plan for your life.

"For I know the plans I have for you," declares the Lord, "plans to prosper you and not to harm you, plans to give you hope and a future," (Jeremiah 29:11 NIV).

The Bible is clear. There is an expected end, a destiny full of promise for your life. Your destiny is not a hit-or-miss game of chance. Great purpose is assigned to your life. Join me on this journey, as we explore the path of faith and obedience, laden with God's promises for your life. Through this book you will gain insight on how to persevere and navigate this ever-changing adventure called life.

Your destiny is not a hit-or-miss game of chance.

It is my sincere hope that this book will inspire, challenge and encourage you, to rise above any adversity you encounter and walk out the prescribed path for your life. I hope that it will serve as a roadmap of sorts, providing practical keys to unlock and open strategies for victory in every area of your life. Let the journey begin.

Chapter 1: Reflections

July 2011 rolled in with blazing heat and violent summer storms. An unrelenting stretch of ninety degree days; left many people feeling drained and weary from the heat. The parched ground seemed to cry out in utter protest at the brutal heat and disappearance of rain. The weather seemed to mirror the difficult season I faced in my own life. I was still reeling from one of the biggest decisions I ever had to make. I had worked ten years as a psychiatric nurse with a great paying job, wonderful benefits, and friends, but after a dream in the night, I walked away from it all and stepped out into a whole new world.

I remember it so vividly. January 3, 2011, I stood on the concrete steps of the bustling psychiatric clinic, for the last time. A single tear escaped my eye. I brushed it away with my sleeve and looked down at the concrete steps, trying to push back the flood of memories that sought to engulf me. A few stray tears dropped to the stairs below my feet. This job had been a home away from home to me; a place where I transformed from a new nurse; into a young wife and later into a mother of two.

The relationships forged in this place were closer than casual co-worker formalities. We were a heroically brave team of four nurses and three doctors, together facing the wicked shadows and secrets of life, day in and day out. Together we entered the dark shadows of repressed abuses, ravaged emotions, and unthinkable acts, and we pulled traumatized victims out of hiding and into a place of hope, refuge and safety. This place was a haven, a refuge of sorts to those whose minds and emotions tormented them savagely.

Over the years, the medical team grew to love one another. We shared so much: family stories, pictures of new babies and grandkids, weddings and baby showers filled our lives. We even shared lunches and dinners outside of work. We cried during personal tragedies and supported each other day in and day out. All the while, the daily heroics of survival brought us closer and closer together. We faced life together, and for ten challenging yet rewarding years, this had been my home away from home.

> ***Together we entered the dark shadows of repressed abuses, ravaged emotions, and unthinkable acts, and we pulled traumatized victims out of hiding and into a place of hope, refuge and safety.***

Some call it work, but, for us, it was life. Somehow the term "work" did little to adequately capture the realm in which we lived. We shared weekend updates and funny stories over steaming cups of coffee and tea in the break room. Unit luncheons and impromptu runs to the bakery brightened our days. These lighthearted moments helped to ease the grim reality of the child psychiatric world. It was never an easy feat to witness children in varying states of grief and distress. Debilitating mental illnesses sought to rob them of their joy and youthful existence. It was agonizing to see children suffering silently while they peered at you, helplessly incapable of conveying the true origin of their torment, yet desperately wanting to be free.

Working in the child psychiatric field was heart-rending and carried great risk for weariness and burn-out, so we strived to find fibers of light amidst the complex tapestry of our reality. I don't know if you have ever seen a child suffering emotionally or physically, but it is agonizing to witness.

I could only withstand so much of seeing helpless children ravaged by abuse, depression, paranoia and eating disorders that were eating away at their souls; without feeling helpless and at a loss. Mere medicine in the psychiatric realm where we dwelled seemed greatly insufficient, like a series of tiny Band-Aids placed on the deep wounds of these children. Yet, this was my world, day in and day out, for ten years. Many days, we felt helplessly insufficient, we knew that more needed to be done; for the young lives we wished we could evict from the deceitful maze of torment that held them captive. Sad were the cases we saw daily, victims of unthinkable crimes, some far too torturous to speak aloud. This was our grim reality.

Standing on the Promises

I stood on the steps that I had ascended and descended thousands of times, for the last time. The faces of friends, who had become family, passed through my mind and caused my heart to tighten. I sucked in a deep breath and exhaled loudly, trying to muster a few ounces of bravery, and I stepped forward away from the steps and toward my car. As I walked to my car, I turned around one final time and looked at the familiar building that had served as a cocoon for my metamorphosis, and captured so many of my tears and fears. With a final smile, I waved good-bye.

After years of working in the psychiatric nursing field, I knew well that closure was important. Though I was only leaving a job, the place it held in my heart ran much deeper than that. Over the years, I had worked with several hundred children and adolescents with varying degrees of mental illness, substance abuse issues and those struggling to deal with the atrocities of abuse. These were some of the ones I thought about while taking those final steps into my new assignment. I whispered a prayer for "my kids." That's what I called them, "my kids." The co-workers I had grown to love were like family. Tears betrayed my eyes and streamed down my face. My heart burned. I lifted my chin and fought to hold back the flood of emotion that was demanding to break forth.

As I walked away from a decade of caring for others, I knew my assignment was changing. I had a six-month-old and a four-year-old at home who needed me, and truth be told, I needed them. My husband, had been running and managing our trucking and transportation company alone, and now I would have the privilege of helping him. Leaving work was one of the hardest things I had ever done. Just thinking about it even now causes tears to burn in my eyes and brings back a wealth of fond yet challenging memories.

Six months later...

August 2011, I was well into my leap of faith journey away from employment, but my world was no less uncertain. Many days I wondered *"who leaves a great paying job in the middle of an economic recession?"*

The skyrocketing price of gasoline caused my stomach to churn as I realized I had completely walked away from the security of my career. Those months that followed my departure from employment, tested me and my family relentlessly and stretched us beyond our natural capacity to believe. We were stretched to a place beyond our own ability to provide for our family and to a place where we had to completely rely on and trust God. If you have never walked on these waters of uncertainty before let me tell you that it is no easy feat. Some days I thought I would buckle under the weight of uncertainty and run, waving a white flag, back into the safe arms of employment. Fear and doubt plagued my thoughts and caused insomnia to creep into my life. I thought this would be an easy transition. I never anticipated the worry, anxiety, fear and doubt that visited me daily.

> ***If you have never walked on these waters of uncertainty before let me tell you that it is no easy feat.***

The season was beyond challenging. Many days I wrestled with that one word question, *"Why?" Why did God instruct me so clearly, yet vaguely, to leave my job? Didn't He know that America and much of the world was in the midst of an ugly recession and hoards of people were jobless and desperately seeking work?*

I felt silly that I had walked away from a great paying job that provided my family with ample security and provision. Silly is putting it mildly; I felt downright foolish for walking away from such sound stability when everyone around me seemed to be in desperate search of jobs and better jobs. To make matters worse, I had no other job lined up. I left work, much like Abraham, because the Lord said "go." Go where? I had no idea.

Yet, somewhere deep in my heart I knew that God was up to something, and I did not want to forfeit or interfere with His master plan for my life, so my husband and I waited and endured, fighting to stay financially and emotionally afloat and growing increasingly curious about what the future held. I knew that there was something God had for me to do. I knew that there was purpose and even promises assigned to my life. Yet, I felt like I was stumbling haphazardly through life, hoping to one day stumble upon my purpose, though I did not know what it was.

Standing on the Promises

The place that we were in certainly tested our faith. It is in such places that faith is tested, proved and refined. Such places of testing must not be overlooked or undervalued. Have you ever found yourself in a place where you faith is stretched? Know that God is preparing you for something, and your preparation process must not be abbreviated or circumvented. God is ever at work in your life, even when it does not seem that way.

Through that time of great transition, my family and I learned how to do more than survive. We learned how to soar.

As I reflect on that season it is clearly apparent that God was with me, from the great leap off the mountain of stable employment, through the tumultuous season of testing and having to trust God even when it seemed there was no stable ground to stand on. Through that time of great transition, my family and I learned how to do more than survive. We learned how to soar. We discovered the key that unlocked our fears and ushered us out of that place of instability and into a place of great promise and blessing. The key that changed our lives forever was discovering how to stand upon God's Word and His promises and apply them to every storm, fire and wind of life. We discovered the power of unshakable faith. That key unlocked many doors and ushered us from a place of turmoil, fear and poverty into a place of rich abundance.

However, my journey was not always this faith-filled. There were some rough times along the way. In fact, there were a series of bad decisions and wrong turns that nearly cost me everything, including my life…

Chapter 2: Strike One

I grew up near Amish country in northeastern Pennsylvania. It was the strangest thing. Fifteen miles in one direction, towering buildings and businesses lined city streets. Smoke billowed into the sky from overworked cars and bustling industries. If I traveled fifteen miles in another direction, rolling green pastures greeted me. Fat lazy cows, chickens and pigs and something called silos lined the country roads. An Amish community was located just fifteen miles in another direction. I remember riding through Amish country, time and time again, with curious intrigue. Horse-drawn buggies, black hats, long pants and boots were a daily sight regardless of the season. Ankle-length dresses of a variety of muted colors adorned the women and girls. Long neat braids peeked out of bonnets and dangled happily in the breeze. That is where I grew up, seemingly in the center of three very different worlds. I do not recall what was in the fourth direction, but I grew up in the center of all of it. Each diverse experience played a role in shaping me.

I excelled in school. I made near perfect grades, but school was never a challenge. For the most part I counted the moments until graduation like a juvenile bird, desperately eager to make my escape.

In high school, my seat of choice was towards the back of the class out of direct view of whichever teacher was lecturing. I took haven close to the windows. The windows, I have always been fond of them. Or maybe not the windows, bur the expanse on the other side of those windows. Day after day, I sat by the windows and allowed my imagination to quietly tiptoe over to the window, ease it open, and then swan dive to the waiting world below. That's what I dreamed about day in and day out, the world outside my window. High school was painfully boring to me and I yearned to turn the page and slide into the next chapter of my existence.

High School graduation came and went. Before I knew it, I was just weeks away from leaving home for college. It was time to move to a new state and launch out into the world that had frequented my dreams. I could not wait to dive into the world outside my window. August 1996 finally arrived and I began life as a college freshman. That was the pinnacle of my adolescent imagination. I could fathom nothing greater than college life. College equated to freedom in my tender mind, and freedom was what I wanted. I failed to realize that freedom for a youth who had barely tasted freedom could prove to be challenging and even dangerous, but I didn't care. I was in passionate pursuit of freedom.

Just days before I left for college in North Carolina a run-in with the law nearly brought my immature dreams to a screeching halt. My parents had always instilled words of truth into my life. Those were the words I bottled up and stored on the dusty shelf in the back of my mind and only reached for when absolutely necessary. Yet, on this occasion my mother's words came for me and found me lying face down on the rocky ground amidst a sea of flashing blue lights.

Speeding Towards Disaster

The night was hot, far hotter than it had been and crickets seem to cry out in a summer chorus. A friend dropped by and picked me up for a joy ride and late night dinner. Sure it was late, but I didn't care about the time, besides I was nearly grown and in a matter of days would be leaving for college, launching out in total independence. Well, at least semi-independence considering my parents would be paying for my college education, food, car and probably gas too. Anyway, I was well on my way to self-proclaimed semi-independence and freedom. So that fateful night Eric and I sped through the city going nowhere fast, talking and laughing, reminiscing about the past four years of our lives. We were both recent high school graduates and both dangerously green about the world we were about to encounter.

We sped down the open road, windows open and seats reclined at a defiantly youthful angle. The hazy humid air took my breath away. Eyes

Standing on the Promises

closed, head back, thoughts of the future flooded my mind. We were going so fast but it felt good. The hot wind stung my face like tiny needles, but I fought to stay in that place of euphoria enjoying the thrill of the fast ride. Not a care in the world. Life was good, freedom beckoned me. I was hooked and could not wait to experience independence on a daily basis. For a high school student, freedom is one of the greatest things imaginable. The hot air whizzed through the car and rested on me like a jacket.

A few cruel seconds later everything changed. My immature world and dreams of freedom collided head on with reality as the sound of blaring sirens assaulted my ears. I sat straight up in the car, wondering what was happening. The sirens grew closer. I glanced in the rearview mirror and saw two police cars hot on our trail.

Startled, I turned to Eric, a good friend or so I thought. I expected him to say something comforting or reassuringly confident, but instead he looked terrified, his hands shook violently, and his eyes darted about as he pulled the green '91 grand marquis to the side of the road. The crunch of the worn tires leaving the road and entering the gravel parking lot echoed loudly in my ears.

That's when everything became foggy, though my mind recorded every sight and sound. It seemed like everything shifted into super slow motion. My ears stood at attention, my eyes were probably as wide as silver dollars as my mom often said. Everything sounded menacingly loud even the leaves crunching under the feet of the officers as they approached the car. I heard the wringing of Eric's hands and the grinding of his teeth as he stared forward as though frozen in time, refusing to look in my direction. He wouldn't look at me. Fear gripped me.

My mind raced, desperately trying to make sense of what was unfolding. Nothing made sense. We were just having the best of times. *"What was happening?"* my mind demanded.

The words Eric and the police officers exchanged were unrecognizable to my ears. Their quiet conversation quickly escalated to gruff accusations and boisterous shouting. Within seconds Eric was hauled out of the car by two police officers clothed in blue. He was thrown face down on the rocky gravel. His hands cuffed and rights read to him.

Rights read to him? This was something I had only seen on Saturday nights while watching COPS reruns and eating popcorn with my family! My mind struggled to process the scene around me.

The trunk of the car opened and one of the police officers rummaged through it with a long flashlight, seemingly on a mission to find something. Another officer ran to his car and called for backup. An army of other sirens grew closer and closer. I heard it all. The commotion and shouting, an onslaught of boots racing through the gravel, a flashlight dropped, orders barked. I was still sitting in the passenger seat of the '91 grand marquis. I gripped the seat, eyes tightly closed, praying I would wake up from this awful nightmare. My head was spinning, the dizzying feeling sought to claim my dinner. A feeling of desperation and fear snuck up behind me and caught me around the throat. I fought to make sense of what was happening second by second.

I remember the offensive smell of the dark haired officer with the angry eyes as she opened my car door and ordered me to exit the vehicle. My eyes were already filled with tears as I fought to maintain some semblance of composure. I stared at the ground and it stared back at me. A swarm of police officers in blue had converged on the scene, and surrounded that green grand marquis, like a hive.

A gruff sounding officer instructed me to lie face down on the gravel, sharp rocks pressed into the side of my face. I dropped to the ground without question. There was no time for tears or questions. It all happened so fast, only fear, no terror, as I saw my world slipping away. I remember the pressure of the black boot pressing into my back, as a lady officer dumped the contents of my purse onto the hood of the squad car. She spat nasty words at me as I was face down in silence and utter disbelief.

"What are they looking for?" I wondered naively. "*Don't they know I am a straight-A student? Don't they know I have never been in trouble? Don't they know I am just days away from leaving for college?*" All of these thoughts flooded my mind.

It was at that moment that my mom's words began to echo loudly in my ears. "You must be careful who you surround yourself with because you are known by the company you keep. Honey, always remember, if you lay down with dogs you will get up with fleas."

That last part brought momentary warmth to my heart. I remember my mother proclaiming those words on more than one occasion as I bounced out the front door without a care in the world. I always laughed when she said those words. I never thought those words would find me like this.

"Momma was right." I thought. *"She was right."*

The officers found a package in the trunk. Eric had been transporting drugs. Throughout the entire ordeal Eric never so much as looked at me. He never offered an apology or spoke a single word to me. This was supposed to be my friend! Eric was handcuffed and thrown head first into the back of a blaringly loud Impala. To my horror and utter disbelief, I was, too. That's right. I was, too. Me, a straight-A, never been in trouble young girl, and I was seated in the back of a speeding Impala headed to jail.

We arrived at the police station, my head hung low I was too ashamed to look anyone in the eye. I equally feared someone may see and recognize me. My world seemed to crumble in my hands. I exited the car in handcuffs and entered the police station for questioning. It all seemed like a cruel nightmare. I desperately wanted to scream and wake up from the torturous scene.

Over and over I thought, *"This can't be happening to me!"*

I spent several hours alone with my thoughts in an empty cell. A kind, yet serious looking officer approached me. My eyes rested on the gun at her waist. She opened my cell and ordered me to join her at a small table in the center of the booking station. I followed her silently. She questioned me for about thirty minutes, satisfied that I did not know about the drugs being transported she proceeded to try and talk some sense into me.

I remember her kind motherly words "Honey just what are you doing here? Don't you know that you could go to jail for this? Are you trying to throw away your future? Every decision that you make can impact your future for better or for worse. You must be careful of the company you keep. You had no business being in the car with that guy. We'd been looking for him for a long time."

My head swam as her words surged over me like a high tide. The entire night seemed like a dream. The officer sounded like my mother, even had a warm smile and tender eyes like my mom. Her face was stern, but her eyes were kind. I allowed her words to embrace me and I genuinely heard them. Like I said, I had heard them before. My mother and father never hesitated to instill truth in me, and that night all of their words over the past sixteen years came for me and found me, sitting alone in a jail cell. Finally, I had nowhere to run, nowhere to hide.

The kind officer adjusted the black frame glasses on her nose and stared me in the eyes to make sure her words were hitting home. She let out a sigh and shook her head as a few stray tears journeyed down my face.

Satisfied that she had reached me she spoke, "Well, you can go now."

I looked out the window and saw the sun. The ordeal had lasted all night long. They released me, because my record was virtually spotless. They let me go, with no charges. It was all too much. I could hardly walk away from the police station, because I was so overwhelmed with emotion. I fought to hold back the flood of tears. A combination of fear and relief stirred in my heart. The events of the night replayed in my mind.

That night freedom took on a new meaning in my life. I realized how fortunate I was to walk away from that situation completely free. Well, almost completely free. I knew that the memories of that night would stay with me forever. The thought of freedom still intrigued me, but in a different way. That night I was desperately grateful for freedom.

Chapter 3: Strike Two

Winter break arrived with jubilant cheers and sighs of relief from the student body. A challenging sea of midterms left me feeling depleted and desperately in need of some rest and relaxation. I decided to travel to Maryland to visit Mia, my best friend from childhood. Mia and I grew up together and for many years we were virtually inseparable. For a season during high school, I spent more time at her house than I did my own. I called her mom, "mom" and her family welcomed me as one of their own. My family extended the same love and acceptance to Mia. Though I was attending college a couple states away, our friendship remained intact.

I wanted to spend winter break in Maryland, but did not have a car or friend to catch a ride with, so I bought a bus ticket to Baltimore, MD. No car, no problem. I would take the bus. It seemed easy enough, besides I was grown, a freshman in college. Surely I could navigate a bus ride across a couple states.

I could not sleep the night before the trip. My mind raced. I had never been on a lengthy bus trip like this. Due to the numerous stops and indirect bus route, the usually five hour trip would take twelve to thirteen hours. I was excited about seeing my friend, but nervous about traveling twelve hours on a packed inner city bus with hoards of people I'd never met. It was holiday season and crime had skyrocketed. I knew enough not to travel with a purse and to keep money and valuables well hidden, still this did not totally put my fears at ease.

A friend dropped me at the bus departure station at three a.m. The full moon sat high in the sky, casting an eerie stream of light on my path. The bus was scheduled to leave at 4am and I wanted to make sure I got a seat near the front. The weather was freezing. Icicles from a recent winter storm hung menacingly around the perimeter of the building and on many of the parked buses. The ground crunched beneath my feet, the morning thaw had not yet begun. It seemed that everything was cold including me. The wind-chill had to be below zero. The wind, or the "hawk" as my mom liked to call it, blew fiercely and betrayed the thin lining of my fleece coat. I huddled beside my duffle bag wishing I had donned another layer of clothing. I waited in line with a sea of other people to board the bus.

Fishnets and razor blades

I noticed a strange man and woman standing just a couple feet in front of me. They reeked of cheap wine and cigarettes. They spat slurred angry words at each other's faces. The man towered over the wide-hipped woman. His mangy beard stretched and curled up the sides of his face and got lost in the mess of speckled gray hair atop his head. His beady eyes glared at the woman and darted around searchingly. He scratched at his face with grimy fingernails.

The woman however, could not have been more than five feet tall, but her attitude was as fiery as a ticked off bulldog. She did not back down. That wide-hipped woman wore a purple spandex dress, fishnet stockings, a green velvet pocketbook, and sparkly earrings that danced on her shoulders. A tattoo peeked out of the collar of her coat and stretched across her neck. Her man (or so I assume,) spat venomous accusations at her, but that short fiery woman didn't even flinch. She retaliated with an equally vicious onslaught of filthy words delivered through pops of her chewing gum. Then she looked him up and down and threatened to cut him with a razor blade.

Cut him? Was she serious? I silently prayed that the line would move quickly so that I could hand over my ticket and board the bus. I did not want to be around this fearsome pair a moment longer.

I felt all the color run out of my face onto the icy ground beneath my feet.

Standing on the Promises

It was as though the savage looking couple heard my thoughts. They turned around simultaneously and greeted me with a sinister grin. I felt all the color run out of my face onto the icy ground beneath my feet. I realized the man was missing several teeth including the two important teeth in the front. My mind drifted and I wondered how he managed to eat any food missing that many teeth. He retracted his grin and his menacing icy stare caused the frigid wind to feel ten times colder. My eyes grew wide, I couldn't help it, I was terrified. I know I looked like a scared squirrel frozen stiff in the middle of a busy highway.

The short wide-hipped woman looked me up and down and through pops of her chewing gum let a few nasally words slide out of her mouth. "Hey honey," she said. "Where ya headed?"

I swallowed hard wondering why they cared. My mind raced. *Should I lie, tell the truth, or pretend not to hear her?*

Though it was cold, I could feel droplets of sweat forming on my palms. I gulped and tried to look brave and unnerved, though I fell short pitifully. At that moment the loud speaker crackled and blared into the blustery air.

"All aboard, bus ninety-three is now boarding! Bus ninety-three board now," the operator shouted.

That was all I needed to hear. I grabbed my lime green duffle bag and literally pushed through the crowd and raced to the front of the line to board my waiting bus, leaving the eerie couple behind me.

I handed the driver my ticket and slid into a second row seat, thankful that I secured a seat almost parallel with the driver. I didn't want to know what went down in the rear of overcrowded buses in high crime season, I was determined to sit as close to the exit as possible. I peeked out the window looking for the sinister couple, to my relief they were still waiting for their bus to arrive. Thankfully, they would not be joining me on bus 93. My heart thumped in my chest as I wondered if I had made a mistake by choosing to ride the bus. I tightened my grip on my duffle bag and curled around it using it as a pillow. The best way to pass the miles was to sleep, and that's just what I did.

Twelve long hours later the bus lurched to a stop in Baltimore Maryland. I glanced out of the window at the snow covered cars and streets. A recent snow had left the city draped in a thick blanket of white. There were too many stops to count. We stopped at four fast food joints and three more rest areas while sixty-five chattering adults and antsy kids fidgeted their way up the highway, the trip was tortuous.

How could a five hour car ride take twelve full hours on a bus? I was still baffled, but gathered my bag and stumbled off the overcrowded bus. I stepped into the bus station and was greeted by Mia's exuberant smile and warm hug. The stress of the day evaporated as we exited the bus station and headed for her home.

New Year's Eve

Winter Break was a blast. Reunions with friends from high school, holiday parties, and shopping trips to the mall were highlights. Snowball fights, ice skating and sledding on the remnants of the last snowstorm made this winter break a teenagers' dream vacation. Our days and nights were spent reminiscing, catching up and letting our imagination take us to unknown places as we fearlessly imagined the next chapters of our lives.

Mia and I were closer than ever and a gentle sadness settled in as we realize the end of my visit drew closer. It would soon be time to board that bus and return to college. The weekend before my departure we made plans to attend a happening New Year's Eve party with friends from around the city. December 31, 1996, a date I will never forget. It is a date that will forever be imbedded in my heart.

We dressed for the party with music blasting, ready to bring in the New Year with a bang. Our dates would meet us at the party. We took extra time with hair and make-up, nails, jewelry, all the things ladies love to perfect when they are venturing out for a night of excitement. We headed for the party. I was driving. We filled our time with singing holiday songs and talk about resolutions for the New Year. Everything was going so well.

We stopped at a red light and sat patiently for the light to turn green. My fingers rapped on the steering wheel to the tune on the radio. Festive holiday lights and Christmas decorations lined the streets and adorned houses around us. The weather was pleasant, a far cry from the brutal cold and snowstorms in the previous weeks.

Anticipation welled within me. We were eager to arrive at the party. Suddenly, I heard a sound. I glanced in the rearview mirror and saw a terrifying sight, a speeding car was headed straight for us and it was not slowing down. I opened my mouth to scream, but it was too late. The last thing I remember seeing was the blinding white lights of the speeding car as it neared, impacted and crushed the back of our car like an accordion. We had been rear-ended by a drunk driver on New Year's Eve. Our vehicle was thrown forward into oncoming traffic. I remember the sounds of horns blaring, screeching tires, and cars swerving to avoid us. I remember the sounds of people yelling and scrambling trying to halt traffic and get us out of the car. I remember the sirens of the speeding ambulances.

I remember the concern on the ambulance driver's face. I remember him congratulating me. Things got so bad so fast.

"Just relax," he said. "You are going to be ok. You did a great job. After you all were hit from behind, you steered the crumpled car across the street out of the stream of oncoming traffic. That likely prevented any further accidents. You did a great job," he said. He could not hide the concern in his voice.

I locked eyes with him, searching desperately for a reassuring sign that I was going to be ok. I glanced to my right and saw Mia being loaded into the back of an ambulance with traces of snow still on its roof. The ambulance doors slammed shut and the piercing siren filled the night. That's all I remember before everything faded to black.

Months later at an intense physical therapy session, I took a moment to reflect. Our lives had been miraculously spared. Many who are in motor vehicle accidents or hit by drunk drivers experience a much more tragic outcome. Tremendous gratitude welled within my heart. God had again spared my life. I returned to college a couple weeks later and attended ongoing physical therapy sessions for several months. I was so fortunate. I began to wonder just what God had in store for my life. I felt a great assurance that God had been watching over me far more than I realized. My heart swelled with joy as I looked hopefully towards the future.

Chapter 4: Strike Three

I was stubborn. One would think those past events would have served as a major wake-up call for me, but I was downright stubborn. I passed on the opportunity to make wiser decisions continued down the same dangerous path. I made it through my first year of college rather unscathed, but year two brought with it a world of new opportunities. Somehow I landed a job working in a happening local night club.

Let's establish a few things. As a child growing up in Pennsylvania, my family attended church and Sunday school weekly. I was truly brought up in the church. My parents were deacons and Sunday school teachers, not only did they talk the talk, but they truly walked it. Their lives modeled for me the true meaning Christianity.

My mother had another saying. She was quite good at dishing out the perfect saying at just the right time. She would often look at me and say, "Your father and I have laid the foundation, now what you do with it is up to you. We have laid the foundation right."

I knew what she meant. My father equally worked to instill in me the uncompromising commitment to do what is right in every situation. However, just two years into my college existence, I was building a house through my actions and decisions that was destined to crumble. I knew about God, but I lacked any measure of a personal relationship with Him. I had a major encounter with the Holy Spirit at the age of ten, but I suppose I had stored that neatly on the same dusty shelf, where my parent's words of wisdom and truth took up daily residence.

Back to the nightclub, working at the night club was a college student's dream! Fast money and faster times! I worked Friday and Saturday nights and made more money from those two nights than I did working two weeks at my regular job. Like I said a college students dream. I went to work when the sun went down and left at any number of wicked hours of the morning. I was never a "dancer," but I worked in the nightclub as an underage bartender. I often laughed. I couldn't drink alcohol legally, but I was selling it faster than water. I loved the nightclub life and it loved me. I was the bartender everyone knew and loved. My social status soared and I often felt like a local celebrity as I walked the streets of campus.

I became so consumed in the nightclub life that college was a mere afterthought. I went to class when I had enough energy to get up or didn't have an event to help promote. I studied when there was nothing else possible to do. I had recruited my college roommates and together we worked the nightlife. The club saw a surge in attendance partly because of the great advertising we did on campus, and as a result I soon got a promotion.

The club owner trusted me and gave me a new job description. I became "the money girl." I was moved from the back of the nightclub to the front door and given the coveted duty of greeting the patrons and collecting the money. I could not believe how fortunate I was to receive such a promotion. Night after night, I dressed the part and came to work, filled with anticipation. Each night, I greeted the sea of eager gentlemen and jealous ladies, who all wondered how I snagged the best seat in the house. A team of bouncers surrounded me nightly as I worked the front and served as an austere hostess. Life was grand. I dodged phone calls and questions from my parents and plunged deeper into the high-octane world of the nightlife. I didn't realize I had completely lost sight of my college hopes and dreams. I still attended college, but it was definitely not a priority.

Facing Death

One night, everything changed. It was a fall night. The air was crisp but not too cold. The trees bristled as the wind whipped through their increasingly bare branches. It had rained earlier. Brakes squealed and squeaked and the sound of tires racing down the wet macadam filled my ears. I arrived at work early. The parking lot was still empty. I stepped over puddles of standing water, refusing to muddy my black knee-high boots.

Joel, one of my favorite bouncers, greeted me at the door with a big grin. Joel looked like a massive football player. He was menacingly big, but had an even bigger heart. He saved his smile for close companions, but when he smiled you couldn't help but chuckle. His smile seemed to come from somewhere deep within and to engulf all in its path. I liked Joel. I felt safe around him.

"Good evening, Miss Christina," Joel greeted me with that good ole southern drawl.

"Hi Joel," I replied returning his smile.

"It is going to be a good night," he announced.

"Yes, Joel. I hope that it is." I began checking on various areas and setting up for the usual weekend parties.

The night proceeded uneventfully. A sea of eager-eyed college-aged lovers of the night-life filled the place and plunged into the intoxicating groove of the music. The crowd was larger than normal, a great night's revenue. Besides the rain, it was shaping up to be a great night, or so I thought. As we neared the end of the night, the flow of people did not stop, more and more entered the club. The music blared, cars rolled by, the dance floor was covered and the bar without an open seat. It was lively and everyone seemed to be enjoying themselves.

Several males were gathered outside the nightclub sitting on their cars and drinking. This was not unusual. Before long those males started to argue. The arguing escalated to shouting and threats and soon a confrontation was underway. From inside the club we heard the tell-tale sounds of a parking lot brawl, angry shouting, graphic language, and the frightening sound of bodies being tossed against parked cars. The bouncers, who usually guarded me and the safe of money, ran outside to intervene in the escalating showdown.

I sat quietly awaiting their return. A few bartenders stood nearby and waited with me. We were relieved that no gun shots were heard, as this occasionally happened in a bad brawl. We talked casually while waiting for the bouncers to return.

Suddenly, the doors to the nightclub were thrown open and in stormed a huddle of fierce-looking men. Ski masks covered their faces, guns were drawn. The assailants scanned the club like animals on the prowl and abruptly turned in my direction. To my horror, they headed straight for me. Two carried pistols and one a large shot gun. There was no denying it; they were headed straight for me. For a split second, I thought I was dreaming. They moved quickly as though on a strategic mission. They moved stealthily as though on a strategic mission. Fear paralyzed me. I tried to run, but my body would not cooperate. I couldn't scream, I wanted to but I couldn't. I opened my mouth, but no sound came out. They came closer. I wished I was invisible. It all happened so fast. *Why was this happening to me?* I gripped the seat of the chair I was perched on as though it could save me. The bouncers were still outside breaking up the fight.

I knew working in a nightclub was not what I should be doing. I knew my parents would have been disappointed. I had boldly defied the truth that had been instilled in me from such an early age. At that moment I thought about my family, my parents and my brothers. *Was this it for me?* I thought I would go on to do so much after college and now I was staring death in the face or, rather death was staring me in the face! Death was coming for me and I was too frozen with fear to run. The menacing crew with drawn weapons drew closer. They were only several feet away, but I could not pry myself from that seat. See, the problem was the safe containing all of the money was right under my high-back chair. The robbers had to go through me to get to the safe of money. I knew that and unfortunately they knew it, too.

The assailants were so close. I knew it was over for me. The sound of gunshots rang out! I tried to scream and this time my voice did not fail me. A piercing sound escaped my throat as I felt the impact to my chest. I flipped over backwards out of the high-back chair and hit the cement floor hard.

The sound of gunshots rang out! I tried again to scream and this time my voice did not fail me.

While I lay on the cold wet cement floor, I had a chance to do some thinking. Finally, after all of the running, all of the partying and rebelling I was forced to slow down and think. At this point, I had no other choice. Stretched out on the floor, tears streamed down my face, and I realized my life had not been going the way I imagined. All of those adolescent dreams of a fairytale life seemed to be slipping away. I was falling short in so many ways, mistake after mistake and bad decision after bad decision. I was throwing my life away and I knew it. Three strikes are written about in this book, but my life's list included many more poor decisions that jeopardized my future. As I lay on the cold wet floor, finally God had my full and undivided attention.

My mind drifted. Memories from my childhood resurfaced clearly. I remembered the time I fell off the second-story balcony of my childhood home. My mind drifted, I could see myself standing on that green and white balcony. The chipped green and white paint on the balcony railing felt rough in my hands. I used to chip away the paint with my fingernails. I remembered how I loved to stand on that second story balcony and look out at the world. Momma scolded me frequently, because I would go up there and lean over the railing. She forbade me from going up there, fearing that I would fall.

I remembered the day it happened. I secretly went up to the balcony. I loved the feel of that rough green and white paint beneath my fingers. I rubbed my hands over the railing memorizing the pattern with my fingers. The breeze blew gently in my hair and I leaned forward to get a better view. That was the last thing I remember. Suddenly, the balcony railing broke and I fell off the balcony, down to the concrete steps.

It was quite a fall from the second-story balcony. Yet, some miraculous way, I sustained no major injuries. In fact, I was not hurt at all. I fell from a second-story roof balcony onto the concrete stairs below. My parents found me lying peacefully at the bottom of the concrete stairs. They rushed to my rescue, wondering frantically if my body was badly broken or worse. But it wasn't. When they asked me what happened, I plainly told them the truth.

"I fell of the balcony…and an angel caught me." No scars, no injuries, no pain. An angel caught me.

And so I got things right with God. I have heard it said, that when facing death many people have a change of heart and get things right with God. Well, I can't speak for others, but that is certainly what I did. I prayed something I seldom did in that season of life, but in the face of death there was no other option. My carefree joyride on the speedway called life had come to a screeching halt.

I lay on the cement floor trembling and shaking. I was not ready to die, although death was staring me in the face and had struck me viciously in the chest. I knew this could be the end for me and my youthful endeavors could be extinguished prematurely. I searched my mind for something to hold on to, as it seemed that everything else was slipping away. I remembered well my father and mother teaching me about God and how He loved me unconditionally despite mistakes. That truth came for me and found me lying on that cold wet cement floor. I reached for that truth and clung to it with everything in me.

I shifted my focus from the scene around me to God. I asked God to forgive me for the rebellion and disobedience and I asked Him to save my life. I begged Him to hold back death that was knocking violently at my door, and let me live. Tears streamed down my face as my heart cried out to God. I did not know if I would make it through the night, but I knew I had gotten things right with the One who held my future, and even the world in His hands. While I lay on that cold wet floor, I could hear the gunmen. They were right over me collecting the money from the safe. Hard as I tried I could not stop the tears from running down my face, but I dared not move or even breathe for fear that they would shoot.

Finally, after what seemed like an eternity I heard their look-out man yell, "Here they come, we gotta go now!"

I heard the sound of their boots against the rain soaked ground as they ran frantically out of the club. I remember the crashing slam of the door as they exited. I remember the screeching sound of the tires as their vehicle sped away into the night. I remember the feel of a hand on my shoulder as people ran over to see if I was alive.

The gunmen left and to my amazement I was able to sit up. I checked myself out expecting the worse. There was no blood. My chest hurt deeply, but there was no gunshot wound. I was surrounded by people all asking if I was ok. Half in disbelief half in amazement I realized that I seemed to be ok. Several people helped me to my feet.

A few bartenders witnessed the event and filled in the missing details. The gunmen did open fire and shoot in my direction at close range. However, all of the bullets went around me, not a single bullet hit me. The guy with the shotgun swung his forearm hitting me in the chest, which sent me flying backwards off the high-back chair. That was the impact I felt. I stayed on the ground motionless so they did not attack me any further.

Hearing the details of this brush with death mixed with the emotions of the night was more than I could handle. I dropped to my knees and buried my face in my hands. The tears overtook me and I shook like a sobbing child, thanking God for saving for my life. I relived the near death encounter, over and over, in my mind. Suddenly, the childhood memory of the green and white balcony flooded my heart. Years before, I fell off the balcony and surely could have been hurt or killed.

The words I spoke so matter-of-factly to my parents filled my ears, "I fell off the balcony, and an angel caught me."

As I kneeled on that wet nightclub floor, I knew beyond the shadow of any doubt that an angel had been with me that night. I realized that though the bouncers were drawn outside strategically to break up the fight, God had not left me alone. He had positioned heavenly guards to cover me and keep me from harm. I knew in my heart that an angel had covered me and kept the close range bullets from hitting me.

Wake-up!

There are moments in our lives which can with great certainty be defined as a wake-up call. This was clearly one of those moments. Unlike my previous brushes with danger, this time I listened. I was shaken from my immature state of invincibility and jostled into a wide-eyed existence. I realized that my future was slipping away and it was time to take life much more seriously.

In the months following that frightening brush with death, I held true to the promises I uttered while lying on the cold cement floor of that night club. God became my priority. Church, which I seldom attended in college, drew me in weekly. I was curious to know more about this God who seemed to care so much for me, and who protected me multiple times, in the face of certain danger. I longed to know Him and spent hours reading and studying my Bible.

In addition, I took a more serious approach to my academics and future career in nursing. My relationship with my parents grew stronger as I had a newfound awareness of their love for me. I realized their prayers and words of wisdom, over the years were some of the very pillars of truth to which I clung, in the worst of times. With this awakening also came a new appreciation for those around me. Tony, a friend from college soon became a closer friend. We dated often. I loved that he shared my new appreciation for life. Our relationship blossomed and we became best friends. Life seemed so much sweeter with someone to share it with. Before long we were married. I can still say today that he is my best friend.

It was the wake-up call moments in my young adulthood that helped me find my way. I could have died that night in the nightclub or on New Year's Eve 1996 when a drunk driver slammed into the back of my car, but God kept me here for a reason. I realized that, and a growing curiosity spurred me onward. I suddenly knew there was a greater purpose for my life, what specifically, I did not know but there was a reason for my existence. I was committed to giving God my "yes" and following Him wherever He led me.

The Power of "Yes"

Giving God your "yes" can open up a whole new realm of possibilities. That single word "yes" is full of tremendous power and potential. By giving God your "yes" you cross into a new place of surrender, obedience and faith in God. That one word can mean the difference between success and failure, going forward and remaining in the same state for eternity.

The decision to relinquish control and give God your "yes" is the first step on your journey of discovering the more that God has for you.

At some point each of us has a decision to make. Will you say "yes" to God and His perfect will and plans for your life? Or will you continue to hold the reigns of your existence and attempt to navigate your own course. I believe that making the decision to relinquish control and give God your "yes" is the first step on your journey of discovering the more that God has for you. Regardless of where you are in life, regardless of your economic and employment status and regardless of your spiritual condition I assure you that there is more that God has for you. His plans for your life were ordained before you were ever conceived. There is great destiny and purpose assigned to your life.

You are not living a haphazard day by day existence. In order to reap the benefits and fullness of God's blessings for you, your "yes" is required. Yes, represents relinquishing control to the very one who created you and your destiny. It seems simple, but giving up control is often one of the most difficult things for many to do. Say "yes" to His will, say "yes" to His timing, say "yes" to God when you are afraid and do not know how you are going to make it. Your "yes" is the invitation for God to come in and transform your life. When you give God your "yes" He does not come empty-handed. He comes with justice, mercy, grace, unconditional love and so much more. God is waiting for you to yield your will to Him. It should not have to take a series of tragic events or wake-up calls to capture your attention. Lay all fear aside and give God your complete "yes." Allow Him to catapult you forward on the course of your destiny. Too often we try to help God work things out in our lives. Give up control and trust Him completely. Let God be God in your life.

Chapter 5: Simply Amazing

It's easy to get off track. It doesn't take much to veer down the wrong path. Most people do not plan to go out and engage in major acts of mischief, or be a serial bad decision maker. Instead, one questionable choice after another, leads them on a path increasingly distant from where they should be. It is very easy to go left when you should go right, or pause when you should go forward. Tiny missteps such as these can quickly lead you farther and farther away from your providential path of success.

A Revelation of Grace

After the third strike, I realized I had some tough decisions to make. I could continue spiraling out of control, or I could make a change for the better. One Sunday morning I heard a sermon about God's grace. Pastor Adrian Starks, who serves as senior pastor of World Victory International Christian Center, has always been a powerful messenger of the gospel. No matter the size of the audience, his words of truth reach each on a personal level. He is known for delivering powerful messages that challenge, ignite, and encourage the masses. This was certainly one of those days.

As Pastor Starks proceeded to preach about God's grace, my mind wandered a bit. I was somewhat unfamiliar with this word "grace." Grace, I thought, was something people hurriedly said before devouring their dinner. That was the extent of "grace" as I knew it. I soon discovered that grace was so much more than a brief prayer of blessing before a meal. Grace was precisely what God had given me time and time again, despite my bull-headedness and selfish desire to do what I wanted.

A revelatory moment ensued as Pastor Adrian Starks proclaimed from the platform this stirring description of grace, "Grace, the power of God's love to overcome man's self-defeating actions and those acts of others that are purposed to devastate us. Yet, I am convinced that we won't fully understand the meaning of grace until we are nose to nose with judgment."

My attention was snagged, my heart laid open, as I recounted the series of "self-defeating" actions that plagued my life. Suddenly, I had a new understanding of God's grace and His extraordinary love for all mankind.

"Grace, the power of God's love to overcome man's self-defeating actions and those acts of others that are purposed to devastate us. Yet, I am convinced that we won't fully understand the meaning of grace until we are nose to nose with judgment." -Pastor Adrian Starks

Simply Amazing

God gives His grace to us as a free gift dispensed through the avenue of His immeasurable love for us. Through grace the strikes against us are reversed. Now that is awesome! Through grace our mistakes, blemishes, shortcomings and failures are wiped clean from our life slates. Through grace our marred existence is masterfully fashioned and reshaped by the hands of a loving compassionate God. Through grace we discover that God does not just throw us away when we fail, rebel, disobey Him or even run from Him. When God extends grace to us, it reaches us wherever we are. That is simply amazing. No matter how far we stray from His perfect will and the path of right-living, His grace will find us, reach us and welcome us back with perfect love.

Grace is immeasurable love and favor given by God, though we have not earned it. We can receive His grace anytime and anywhere, it is dispensed as the Lord wills. Through the administration of God's grace we come into a fresh awareness of our sinful nature and God's marvelous love, compassion and all sufficiency. We discover that God truly is our Father and will not cast us away or banish us because of a mistake, no matter how great the error. Even when we knowingly disobey God, we have an opportunity to be a recipient of His perfect love and grace. We are saved and given a fresh start by God's grace. It was God's grace that reached me at age sixteen while sitting in a police booking station. It was grace that prevented me from receiving any criminal charges for my misgivings when they were indeed warranted. It was grace that allowed me to walk away from that frightful encounter, without a blemish on my name or record. By grace I was still able to enter college and pursue God's purpose and plans for my life. That was nothing shy of God's perfect grace. His grace is designed to reach us wherever we are.

The deeper I go into knowing and experiencing God one thing becomes clearer, all that I am is completely a result of God's amazing grace. The grace of God is beyond compare, it is simply amazing. Every failure I experience causes me to humbly become more dependent upon God. Every success I have is a direct result of God's perfect grace. Have I earned it? No. Do I deserve it? No, I do not, but the infinite compassion and wisdom of a loving God offers grace to help us when we need it most.

Let Him Help

God is love and He is full of compassion. God's immeasurable compassion and love is not merely extended to some, but all of humanity, including you. I have often talked with people who find themselves seemingly between a rock and a hard place, facing major decisions with no solutions in sight. It is in this desperate place that many people cry out for help. It is here that many realize their humanity. They reach a place where their own strength, skill and resources prove insufficient and swift divine intervention is needed. A place of great fear for many, because it seems they have run out of options.

Many feel this is a horrible place. I say it is a very good place. It is a divine place where we should acknowledge and realize that our sufficiency is not of ourselves, but our sufficiency is of God (2 Corinthians 3:5). God wants to be involved in every facet, chapter and decision in your life. He wants to help you navigate through this journey called life; the hills, valleys and every place in-between. He wants you to realize that you cannot make it on your own. Truthfully, you need God's help to be successful and victorious in life and you should welcome that help. Do not reserve God's help for times of distress and troubles. Invite Him to help you and release His grace in your life on a daily basis.

"Yet the Lord longs to be gracious to you; therefore He will rise up to show you compassion," (Isaiah 30:18 NIV).

Just Ask

I will never forget the numerous times that I found myself at a crossroads. I remember well the feelings of fear, despair and helplessness as I searched through the rolodex in my mind desperately seeking an answer or a way out. When I came up void of any solutions I resorted to calling on God for help. Why do we do that? Why do we fail to invite God into the details and decisions of our lives from the start? Why do we wait until a problem arises before we seek God for guidance and help? Far too often we live life with an "I can do it myself" attitude. I believe many people are raised to be self-sufficient. Independence is culturally correct and applauded in many countries. However, we must also recognize that depending on God is vitally important.

Pride causes many to eliminate God from their decision making processes, calling on Him only as a last resort. Don't wait. Include God in every aspect of your life. Corporations pay great amounts of money to receive advice and strategies from industry leading consultants. That's great, but when was the last time you consulted God. When was the last time you asked Him for advice, strategy and direction? It won't cost you a penny. I challenge you to do that on a consistent basis. Seek the Lord for direction and insight. It is one of the secrets of discovering your purpose (Jeremiah 33:3). It can be summed up in two simple words, "just ask." Just ask Him. It really is as simple as it sounds. If you ask the Lord something and He does not answer right away, do not give up. Remain faithful in that place of waiting on Him to answer. I think you will be pleasantly surprised what the Lord reveals to your heart.

Standing on the Promises

A Humble Heart Beckons Grace

If you are one who feels unworthy and overwhelmed at the thought of receiving God's grace, then you are in perfect heart position to receive it. A humble heart beckons God's grace. Please understand grace is not something that you earn. It is given by God as a free gift. God bestows grace upon us with great love and compassion and brings restoration in our circumstances, even when we fail to involve Him initially. Everything about our relationship with God depends upon us trusting Him in faith, by resting in His grace.

"For by grace you have been saved through faith, and that not of yourselves; it is the gift of God, not of works, lest anyone should boast," (Ephesians 2:8-9 NKJV).

The scene of the cross was the ultimate demonstration of love. God sent His beloved son to apply perfect love to a sin-sick world. That is the same love God has for you and me. Every time you fall short or make a mistake, remember the cross and thank God for His grace and compassion, because at the cross is where the price for every sin was paid in full! That was the ultimate act of grace and love, greater grace we have not known!

"Greater love has no one than this, that he lay down one's life for his friends," (John 15:13 NIV). God's grace does not depend on your efforts or works, it totally depends upon God. He said to Moses, "I will have mercy on whom I have mercy, and I will have compassion on whom I have compassion For by grace you have been saved through faith, and that not of yourselves; it is the gift of God, not of works, lest anyone should boast.," (Romans 9:15-16 NKJV). Grace does not depend on man's desire or effort, but as God wills.

At times your decisions and actions may miss the mark, ending in failure and disappointment, but you cannot remain in that place of disappointment and discouragement.

But he said to me, "My grace is sufficient for you, for my power is made perfect in weakness. Therefore I will boast all the more gladly about my weaknesses, so that Christ's power may rest on me. That is why, for Christ's sake, I delight in weaknesses, in insults, in hardships, in persecutions, in difficulties. For when I am weak, then I am strong," (2 Corinthians 12:9-10 NIV).

Always understand that your failures and weakness are no match for the grace and love God has for you. No matter what you are facing God's grace is greater. At times your decisions and actions may miss the mark, ending in failure and disappointment, but you cannot remain in that place of disappointment and discouragement. You must come to the end of yourself and call out to God. Then God will release strength and the ability to persevere and overcome whatever obstacle you are facing. As you are enraptured by God's grace, time and time again, your love and trust in God should deepen. One of the best things you can ask for is God's grace and compassion to abound in your life.

Coming Home

The story of the prodigal son in Luke Chapter 15 is familiar to many. In part, it is the story of a rebellious son who rejected his father's upbringing. The younger son asked his father to give him his portion of the family estate as an early inheritance. Once received, the son promptly set off on a long journey to a distant land and wasted his fortune on wild living. When the money ran out, a severe famine hit the country and the son found himself in dire circumstances. He took a job feeding pigs. He became so destitute that he even longed to eat the food assigned to the pigs.

The young man finally came to his senses, and remembered his father. In humility, he recognized his foolishness, and returned to his father to ask for forgiveness and mercy. Not until he was confronted with failure and despair did he return home, repentant and willing to do anything to win back his father's favor. To the son's surprise he was honorably welcomed without question, back into his father's loving and forgiving arms. No amount of time, no amount of betrayal, and no amount of rebellion could stand in the way of the father's unconditional love for his returning son. He was welcomed with love and celebration.

"For this son of mine was dead and has now returned to life. He was lost, but now he is found," (Luke 15:24 NLT).

The father, who had been watching and waiting, received his son back with open arms of compassion and unconditional love. This truly reflects the picture of God's unconditional love for mankind. Oh, God's love for you is beyond measure! The father in this parable was overjoyed by the return of his lost son and ran to greet him! What a display of love. The father did not sit in his living room waiting casually for his son to return. The Bible says he was looking for his son. When the father spotted his son afar off, he ran to greet him. This reflects God's love described in James 4:8, "When we draw near to God, He will draw near to us."

> When he [the prodigal son] came to his senses, he said, 'How many of my father's hired servants have food to spare, and here I am starving to death! I will set out and go back to my father and say to him: Father, I have sinned against heaven and against you. I am no longer worthy to be called your son; make me like one of your hired servants.' So he got up and went to his father, but while he was still a long way off, his father saw him and was filled with compassion for him; he ran to his son, threw his arms around him and kissed him. "The son said to him, 'Father, I have sinned against heaven and against you. I am no longer worthy to be called your son, but the father said to his servants, 'Quick! Bring the best robe and put it on him. Put a ring on his finger and sandals on his feet. Bring the fattened calf and kill it. Let's have a feast and celebrate. For this son of mine was dead and is alive again; he was lost and is found.' So they began to celebrate. (Luke 15:17-24 NIV).

Immediately, the father turned to his servants and asked them to prepare a giant feast in celebration. Likewise, I believe God is well pleased when those who have strayed return wholeheartedly to Him. In fact, Jeremiah 3:14 explains that "God is married to the backslider." Even if you turn away from God and try to divorce Him, He will not forsake or leave you, and you always have the opportunity by grace to come running back to Him.

However, everyone was not thrilled when the prodigal son returned home to such an honorable welcome. The older brother was not one bit happy when he discovered a party going on to celebrate his younger brother's return. The father tried to dissuade the older brother from his jealous rage explaining, "You are always with me, and everything I have is yours."

You must realize that everyone may not be able to understand and appreciate the unmerited favor upon your life. Some may even contest it and resent it. Look to God, not man for affirmation and approval. Do not be so concerned with the opinions and approval of man. It is God, not man, who places the signet ring of favor and reward, upon the hand He chooses. God is the Master of restoration and He has the final say concerning your life.

The older son struggled to understand why one who had demanded his inheritance prematurely, ran away and squandered it all living a life of waywardness and selfishness, could be restored instantaneously and welcomed lovingly back into the arms of his father. That is the picture of God's perfect love and grace for all. It does not matter where you have gone, what you have done or what you have squandered. It does not matter how far you have strayed, you can be restored in an instant! The power of God's grace is simply amazing! Sure, there may be consequences for your actions, but that does not negate the extension of God's love and grace for your life.

A Revelation of God's Love

"For I am convinced that neither death nor life, neither
angels nor demons, neither the present nor the future, nor
any powers, neither height nor depth, nor anything else in

all creation, will be able to separate us from the love of God that is in Christ Jesus our Lord," (Romans 8:38-39 NIV).

There is nothing you can do that would cause God to push you away and stop loving you.

Are you convinced? Are you convinced that nothing, absolutely nothing is able to separate you from God's love? What an incredible revelation! God loves you so much! It does not matter how many mistakes you have made. Those mistakes and shortcomings cannot separate you from God's perfect love. At times you may feel distant from God, but He is still with you and will not leave you. You must grab ahold of the revelation that nothing is able to separate you from God's love. When you have a revelation of God's great love, you become empowered to help others know and understand the greatness of His love and grace. Romans 8:1 tell us there is no condemnation to them who are in Christ. There is nothing you can do that would cause God to push you away and stop loving you. You must not heap blame and shame upon yourself or banish yourself into a life of punishment and exile. It does not matter what you said, did or who you hurt. Those things may be bad, but they are not bad enough to condemn you from the love, grace and redeeming power of God His promises are still applicable for your life. You still qualify to receive His goodness, blessings and mercy.

Erasing the Past

Stop for a moment and think. Search your mind and your heart. What are some of the worst things (by your standards,) that you have done? I say "by your standards," because God does not rate sin, as people often do. You may believe that some sins are worse or more heinous than others, but in God's eyes, sin is sin. Now, what have you done that brought shame to you or your family? What have you done that if given the chance, you wish desperately that you could undo, reverse or even erase? Was it a stent with drugs? Was it an adulterous relationship? Did you say something that hurt someone terribly and wish you could retract those words? Right now you have opportunity to give that situation to God and allow His restoration power in your life. Give it to God. Repent to God and your sins will be forgiven, washed white as snow as though they never occurred (Isaiah 1:18). It is indeed that simple. Repentance means more than uttering an apology or confessing with your mouth. Repentance is the genuine act of turning away. Turn away from those things, which are contrary to the will of God, return to God and where He desires you to be. He is waiting for your return, just like the father of the prodigal son. There is nothing you can do, nowhere that you can go that will separate you from His love and forgiveness.

You may believe that some sins are worse or more heinous than others, but in God's eyes, sin is sin.

You may think that you do not deserve such extraordinary love and God's grace. That is true for all mankind. Not a single one deserves it, but God does not bestow His love and grace upon you, because you deserve it or earned it. He gives His love and grace, because He is God and dispenses grace as He wills. The flow of grace for your life could be halted at any time, so it is never wise to knowingly disobey God believing that grace will cover you. Instead, return to Him as the prodigal son did, and receive the outpouring of favor and mercy that God has reserved for you. The love of God is simply amazing.

Cha... ...d to Stand

You a... ...may seem like that cannot be furt... ...realize it or not, you are called to be a... ...n people allow trials and difficult situati... ...les can easily weary your faith. In the r... ...et that your heavenly father is the One... ...ns were formed. Consider that for a mo... ...were formed. At His word the oceans yi... ...he world was created (Psalm 33:4-9). If ... ...e world, then surely He is able to speak ... ...your situation. God is so much greater ... ...comfort in knowing that He is with you

...ng Adversity

...en you will face various trials and tests. During ... God has passed you by or forgotten you. Does it seem that you... ...ve vanished? Have you been waiting so long that you have given up hope that your dreams will ever be fulfilled? Maybe you have found yourself battling the likes of fear, depression, hopelessness, and discouragement. Life often brings with it challenges of varying degrees that can test your faith to the limit.

Sometimes life seems nothing short of a tumultuous storm sent to blow you off course and drain the life from you. You may be experiencing the aftermath of such a life storm, feeling depleted, disoriented and unsure, which way to go or what to do next. Sometimes you can reach a place where you just feel like giving up, on a job, your marriage, even ministry. This place is a very real place that can resemble the darkest night or a pit of despair. It is during times like this when it seems the storms of life are succeeding in their mission.

The Bible shares that believers can expect to face trials and tests. It comes with the territory and should not be considered unusual to come up against such trials. At times that season of testing can seem never ending. It is easy to become wearied and discouraged.

I remember many times like this, crying out to God for relief from the seemingly relentless season of struggles and adversity. I remember times when I would sit up in the night and cry out to God. *"Why? Why God? Why haven't I seen this situation change? When Lord? When is my answer going to come? When is the season going to change in my favor?"*

> Weariness sought to overwhelm me until I remembered a scripture that I had tucked away in my heart, "Beloved, do not think it strange concerning the fiery trial which is to try you, as though some strange thing happened to you; but rejoice to the extent that you partake of Christ's sufferings, that when His glory is revealed, you may also be glad with exceeding joy," (1 Peter 4:12-13 NKJV).

Think it not strange! As a believer, it is perfectly normal to experience fiery trials. You should not be surprised when such situations arise. The Bible says don't think it strange. The purpose of tests and trials according to 1 Peter 4 is to test you and prove you. You are not enduring in vain, there is purpose assigned to every test. There is purpose for your pain. Rest assured, it is normal to experience fiery trials and though they do not feel good, they are for your good. That is critically important to remember, fiery trials do not feel good, but they are for your good, they are for your making.

Rest assured, it is normal to experience fiery trials and though they do not feel good, they are for your good.

Standing on the Promises

Trials come to make you stronger, to test, prove and refine your faith and obedience. Everything that you go through is for a purpose. God promises to not put more on you than you can bear, but let's be real it does not always feel that way. Sometimes it may feel like you are not going to make it. However, 1 Peter 4:13 reveals the appropriate response to trials and challenges, you must rejoice. Even in the midst of trying circumstances rejoicing is in order and will help transform your situation. When you rejoice your focus shifts from the circumstance back to God. When you rejoice in the Lord, your focus should shift from the problem to the problem-solver! God alone is able to deliver you out of every trial (Psalm 34:19).

Keep On Standing!

"Put on the whole armor of God that ye may be able to stand against the wiles of the devil. For we wrestle not against flesh and blood, but against principalities, against powers, against the rulers of the darkness of this world, against spiritual wickedness in high places. Wherefore take unto you the whole armor of God that ye may be able to withstand in the evil day, and having done all, to stand. Stand therefore, having your loins girt about with truth, and having on the breastplate of righteousness; and your feet shod with the preparation of the gospel of peace" (Ephesians 6:11-15 KJV). Verse 13 says "and having done all, to stand, stand therefore." That's it right there. "And having done all, to stand, stand therefore."

Beloved, keep on standing! After you do all that you can, then stand and keep on standing. You may have prayed, fasted, cried, and exhausted every resource. Sometimes you reach a point where there is nothing else you can do. Maybe someone you love is sick and you have prayed, you have fasted, the doctors have done all they can, and you find yourself in a place where there is nothing else that can be done. Or maybe you need a financial miracle, and you do everything you know how to do to try and work out the situation, and you still come up short. Ephesians 6 tells us "and when you have done all that you can do, then stand, stand therefore." In other words, stand and keep on standing. Put the situation in God's hands and continue to stand in faith.

You mean to tell me that everything is going awry. A major miracle is long overdue and the Word of God says to stand. Just stand? Yes! That is precisely what I am telling you. Let's expose the misconception. Many think of standing as just standing still and doing nothing. On the contrary, standing is a spiritual weapon that is laden with explosive power.

The word stand comes from the Greek word histemi meaning to be steadfast, unmovable, firm, to refuse to be moved or to be set. When something is set, it is fixed. For example when a judge issues a ruling that cannot be overturned it is said that the ruling stands, it is established or set.

Ephesians 6 gives the instruction to "stand." So, where should you take your stand? Ephesians 6:13-14 references feet being shod with the preparation of the gospel of peace or the Word of God. Shod comes from the word shoe. It means for something to be covered completely, like with a shoe. In essence, God's Word should become your shoes. Everywhere that you go, your feet should be completely covered in the Word of God. In other words you are to stand on God's Word and walk therein. Every step that you take should be in agreement with God's will and His Word. As you stand upon the truth of God's Word and walk in the Word, peace will flood your situation, because you are no longer standing on shaky ground. God's Word cannot fail. Choose to stand on God's Word in every situation. It is a sure place. When your feet are planted firmly on the truth of God's Word they are planted on something that cannot fail.

Your Heart Must Stand

To stand on God's Word involves much more than your feet. It is a matter of the heart. In essence your heart must be trained to stand on the promises of God. Your heart must be set, firm and steadfast upon what God has spoken, even in the face of opposition and overwhelming circumstances. In Exodus 14:13-14 the people of Israel were being led out of Egypt by Moses. Pharaoh and his army were hot on their trail. The Red Sea was in front of them and a sea of soldiers behind them. They faced overwhelming obstacles on all sides. It seemed all hope was lost and the people began to panic. They began to cry out and accuse Moses of bringing them out there to die.

Moses said to the people, "Do not be afraid. Stand still, and see the salvation of the Lord, which He will accomplish for you today. For the Egyptians whom you see today, you shall see again no more forever. The Lord will fight for you, and you shall hold your peace," (Exodus 14:13-14 NKJV).

Why did Moses tell the people to stand firm and be still? Was he talking about their feet or their physical movement? I believe "stand firm" addressed their hearts rather than their feet. Remember, to stand can mean to be steadfast and unmovable, but at that moment the Israelites were terrified and wavering. They had already started to retreat back to the captivity of Egypt in their hearts. At the first sign of adversity they wanted to go back. The Israelites were scared and doubtful, the situation looked hopeless and their faith started to fail. The situation looked grim and their hearts were terribly afraid. Moses responded and spoke to the Israelites. His words changed their stance. Moses spoke to their wavering hearts. He commanded their hearts to stand still and watch God deliver them. Moses commanded their hearts and their faith to stop wavering and stand still on the word of God. He commanded their hearts to be steadfast and firm upon what God had promised them. When your heart is steadfast, your mouth will follow. "Out of the abundance of the heart, the mouth speaks," (Luke 6:45). If you feel your faith begin to waver don't wait, take action and command your heart to be steadfast on God's Word. Pray that your faith will not fail and begin to speak in agreement with heaven.

Check Your Stance

In the midst of every situation ask yourself, where are you standing? Are you standing on what you see with your eyes? Are you standing on what your bank account says? Are you standing on what it looks like in the natural? Or are you standing on the Word of God and what He has spoken concerning your life?

In order to stand on the Word and promises of God you need to know the Word of God. To be vaguely aware of the scriptures is not enough. You truly need to know God's Word. The Bible is your divine roadmap. Why attempt to navigate life without it? When you know God's Word, you are positioned for success and apprehending the promises for your life. When you do not know the Word, you are more likely to miss out on promises afforded to you. For example, when you give tithes and offerings faithfully, the Lord will rebuke the devourer for your sake, and He will open up the windows of Heaven and pour out such bountiful blessings that you will not have enough room to receive them all. When you know this promise, you are rightly positioned to apply it to your life, and obtain the reward described in Malachi 3:10. When you know the promises of God, you are positioned to see them fulfilled in your life. Standing is a powerful weapon that will help you to access and apprehend the promises of God for your life.

Think about a situation you are in right now. Where have you taken your stand? Your stance should always be one of faith and standing on the Word of God. When it comes to God's Word and His promises your heart must be steadfast and unmovable, no one should be able to move you from that place of firmly standing on God's truth.

Key 1: The place of standing is the place where you stop wavering, doubting and living in fear.

> 1 Kings 18:41-44 gives the account of Elijah on Mount Carmel. "Elijah said unto Ahab, Get thee up, eat and drink; for there is a sound of abundance of rain." So Ahab went up to eat and to drink. And Elijah went up to the top of Carmel; and he cast himself down upon the earth, and put his face between his knees, And said to his servant, Go up now, look toward the sea. And he went up, and looked, and said, there is nothing. And he said, Go again seven times. And it came to pass at the seventh time,

that he said, Behold, there ariseth a little cloud out of the sea, like a man's hand. And he said, Go up, say unto Ahab, prepare thy chariot, and get thee down that the rain stops thee not."

A three year drought had ravaged the land. Elijah was positioned on Mount Carmel. He had a great view of the land from the mountaintop, but Elijah was not concerned with the view. The Bible describes the interesting position Elijah chose to assume. Although he was on Mount Carmel, Elijah was not surveying the scenery or even looking for raindrops, sure signs that the drought had ended. Instead Elijah crouched low to the ground with his head bent low between his knees. Elijah was not pacing about anxiously. Elijah's faith was strong. Elijah took his eyes off the situation and put them on God. His unusual posture was a posture of faith and prayer. Elijah looked to God alone, not his surroundings.

If Elijah had looked around, he still would have seen drought conditions and the terrible effects of a three year period without rain. The change of seasons had not manifested yet. However, Elijah was not standing on what he could see he was standing on what God spoke to his heart. Likewise, you cannot take your stand upon what you can see. Stand on God's promises even if your circumstances have not yet changed.

In essence to stand can mean to be steadfast and fixed and Elijah's heart was steadfast. He had heard from the Lord. He had heard the sound of rain an indication that the season was changing and the drought was quickly coming to an end. It did not matter that Elijah could not see the rain with his natural eyes. Elijah could see the new season through the eyes of faith. Elijah knew it was coming because God spoke it. He grabbed ahold of that truth with his heart. His faith was unshakable and undeniable. So, even when the servant came back on the sixth time saying, "I went and checked six times. There is still nothing there." Elijah did not even lift his head. He was certain of the word God had spoken. He was certain that God would come through.

Key 2: The place of standing is a sure place.

It is not up to you to know "how" God is going to do it, but you must know and believe that He is God, and He will do just what He said! Doubt must flee in this place of unshakable faith. The place of standing is a sure place of unmovable faith. Elijah knew. On the seventh time, the servant saw that small cloud, the first visible sign that the season was changing, and that rain was coming. However, Elijah did not need to see the cloud, because he already knew God was sending the rain and bringing the drought to an end. Elijah's heart was postured in a place of standing on the promises of God. He would not be moved from that place of believing God. That must be our stance as well. Believe God no matter what!

A Place of Blessing

> Jacob was left alone and a man wrestled with him till daybreak. When the man saw that he could not overpower him, he touched the socket of Jacob's hip so that his hip was wrenched as he wrestled with the man. Then the man said, "Let me go, for it is daybreak." But Jacob replied, "I will not let you go unless you bless me," (Genesis 32:24-26 NIV).

Key 3: The place where you stand on the promises of God is a place of blessing.

Jacob's plight was interesting indeed. Look at the circumstances? Jacob had stolen his brother's birthright, was on the run, and his name meant trickster, but yet there was a promise God had established with Jacob's grandfather before he was ever born. God made a covenant with Jacob's grandfather, and as a result there was generational blessing assigned to his life. Genesis 32:29 says "And he blessed him there." Right there in that place where Jacob took a stand on the promises of God, the angel commanded a blessing upon him. Jacob realized there was blessing assigned to his life and he refused to be moved from that place of believing God. As a result, he tapped into great blessing and favor.

Standing on the Promises

Another account worth exploring is in Daniel 3:16-25, the account of the three Hebrew boys. What a powerful example of ones who stood steadfast and in faith even in the cauldron of great opposition and death. The Hebrew boys took a stand for God and defied the King's order to bow down and worship his idol. They refused to bow down, even though they knew the consequence was death. What was the truth they were standing on?

Shadrach, Meshach and Abednego replied to him, "King Nebuchadnezzar, we do not need to defend ourselves before you in this matter. If we are thrown into the blazing furnace, the God we serve is able to deliver us from it, and he will deliver us from your majesty's hand. But even if He does not, we want you to know, your majesty that we will not serve your gods or worship the image of gold you have set up," (Daniel 3:16-18 NIV).

What a powerful stretch of scripture. The Hebrew boys declared, "Our God is able to deliver us out of the furnace, but even if he does not." What faith! Whether God delivered the Hebrew boys or not, they knew He was able. They were confident in God's ability to deliver them out of the fire, and that is where they took their stand. They did not stand on the notion that this fire is seven times hotter and would surely consume them in an instant. They stood on the truth that God is able to deliver them even from this fiery trial. When the Hebrew boys entered the fire their hearts were standing firm on God's truth. They had a personal relationship with Elohim Yakol, which means God who is able. The Hebrew boys could not be moved or shaken in their faith. They had incredible faith in the face of opposition.

The Hebrew boys had done nothing wrong. They were convicted of serving the one true God and refusing to bow down to an idol. Sometimes we think we are going through a trial or struggle because of sin in our life or God is punishing us. Don't automatically assume that is the case. The situation could be part of the prescribed process for your life.

Key 4: When you stand upon God's Word you are not standing alone.

When you stand upon God's Word, you have the backing of heaven. Even in the midst of the fire, if you stand upon God's Word, then Jesus is standing with you. He is there to help you, intercede on your behalf and see you through every fiery trial. Just as Jesus was beheld as the fourth man moving about in the fiery flames with the three Hebrew boys, likewise He stands with you in the midst of your fiery trials. He does not leave you when the temperature is turned up. It does not matter what is going on around you. It does not matter how bad the situation seems. When you get to the place where your heart is fixed and you are standing on and trusting in God's Word, then you will beckon the King of Kings with your faith. God is summoned to see to it that His Word is performed in your life. Take a moment and ask yourself, where are you standing?

God is summoned to see to it that His word is performed in your life.

Standing in the Fire

Let's talk about the fire. When you find yourself in the fire you need to recognize that God is trying to do something in your life. God does not just put you in the fire to put you there. The fire is a place of purification and refinement. It is not comfortable, but it is the process by which God extracts everything that is not like Him so that He can prepare you for your destiny. So many times people fight their process because it is fiery or intense. Do not attempt to run from your process, instead surrender all to God and allow Him to have His perfect work in your life. He wants to prepare you for your destiny and refine you as silver is refined.

When you find yourself in the fire, rejoice! When the heat is turned up, seven times hotter that is the time to have a praise break, because you better believe that God is doing something in your life! There is destiny assigned to your life and God may choose to take you through the fire, to prepare you for what He has called you to do in the earth.

Pastor Adrian Starks of World Victory International Christian Center in Greensboro, NC shared a powerful revelation that is well worth repeating. He shared, "God is seeking to speak to you out of the fire in your life so instead of

Standing on the Promises

fighting the fire listen and see what God is saying to you." There is a message in every fiery trial and every season of life. God operates with purpose. Look for the message in every situation you face.

What has God spoken over you that you have yet to see manifest? Be reminded today that the Word of God is sure. Psalm 33:11 tells us that "the Lord's plans stand firm forever, His intentions can never be shaken." God's plans, intentions and promises for you stand firm forever! His plans and intentions for you do not waver. If God spoke it, He shall perform it. Be strengthened in your faith today and put a demand on heaven as you take God at His Word. What has He spoken to your heart? What has He shown you? Set it before your eyes. Be reminded of it. Decree it in agreement with heaven. Recognize the power that is within that promise or word from the Lord and pray for it to be released in your life!

Faithfulness

The story of Anna, in Luke 2:36-38, is a perfect picture of faithfulness. Anna had an instruction from God. Her assignment was to pray for the arrival of the Messiah. Anna remained in the temple night and day. Anna was married, but after seven years her husband died and she lived in the temple thereafter. She worshipped the Lord night and day until she was eighty-four years old. Anna had an instruction from God. The Messiah was coming and Anna's assignment was to pray and prophesy until He arrived.

The promise was coming, but before the promise showed up, Anna had to go through something. God said the Messiah was coming so Anna believed He was coming. Had the Messiah come yet? No. Had she seen Him? No, but Anna had a word from the Lord and she prayed into that word for some sixty-six years. Her heart was fixed. She knew God was faithful and would fulfill the promise He had spoken. Her heart was steadfast. She refused to leave the temple. She refused to let doubt get the best of her. Night and day she was waiting on the Messiah to arrive.

She stayed in that place and believed God for that one promise

for sixty-six years or more.

So, what did she do while she was waiting? Anna's heart epitomized steadfastness. She stood on the promise of God so it did not matter that she had to pass through a season of waiting and persevering. She was willing and she was committed to staying in that place until something happened. Anna did not offer a hurried prayer, and then leave her post. Anna stayed in that place and believed God for that one promise for sixty-six years or more. Anna got into a place of faith and she prayed. However, she did not pray casually, she prayed until something happened. Anna fasted until something happened. Night and day, Anna sang until something happened, and she worshipped until something happened.

Anna had a promise and her heart was set. She knew if she just stayed in that place of faith and believing God she would see His word performed in her life. Anna stayed in that place of faith. Some of us get weary after three days and are ready to forfeit. Don't get weary. Keep standing and keep believing. All that God has spoken to your heart is sure. Do not cast away your hopes and dreams. Persevere in faith! Your promise is sure.

Chapter 7: I Will Not Die

Are you familiar with the story of Leah recorded in Genesis Chapter 29? If not, I encourage you to spend some time studying the account. Leah endured great persecution and disappointment before she obtained her promise. It is a story of endurance and hope. Please allow me some literary license as I share how I believe the story unfolded. I imagine it went something like this.

Leah's Plight

Leah's name can mean "misery," and that is the perfect way to describe her life. Leah had a younger sister named Rachel who was a beautiful, shapely, shepherdess. The younger sister Rachel was downright gorgeous, but the Bible describes Leah as simply having…nice eyes. It is clear that Leah paled in comparison to her sister, Rachel, and likely lived in her shadow. Beautiful Rachel won the heart of the eligible bachelor, Jacob, and they were planning to marry. What joy this must have brought to Rachel's heart, and yet this added another burden to the shoulders of Leah. Not only was Rachel far more beautiful, but she was younger and had successfully captured the heart of the most eligible bachelor in town. Young Rachel was about to be married.

However, it was not customary for the younger sister to marry first so their father devised an elaborate plan. On Jacob and Rachel's wedding night, the father deceptively sent Leah to Jacob's tent. Leah went willingly and consummated the marriage in her sister's place, bringing Jacob and Leah into a marriage covenant. What a surprise this must have been to Jacob! It was a deceptive trick, a desperate attempt to marry away an older daughter. What a tragic way for Leah to enter into marriage, a far cry from the hopes of a fairytale romance and wedding. Leah was thrust into the midst of a deceptive plot, but at the same time secretly hoped that things would work out in her best interest. Besides, at least she was married now. One week later Jacob married his true love, the younger sister, Rachel.

Imagine what life was like for Leah. Jacob loved Rachel, but he was bound to Leah through an underhanded trick. In the text there is no indication that Jacob loved Leah, but they had consummated the marriage and were joined together in that binding covenant. Their relationship was borne out of obligation rather than love. Jacob and Rachel likely despised Leah for infringing upon their love relationship. Leah was unloved, rejected, alone, an outsider in her own home. She was "the other woman," void of love and appreciation, surrounded with scandal. She wanted to be loved and cherished. She wanted to experience the joys of family. She wanted to be a good wife. Instead a veil of shame and rejection followed her everywhere.

Leah was a sturdy woman, good in the kitchen and the field. Yet, nothing she did could touch the blossoming love that consumed Jacob and Rachel. Leah was an outsider in her own marriage. Yet, there was a quandary. The younger sister, Rachel, loved Jacob but her womb was coldly barren. Rachel desperately wanted to give Jacob children, but her womb would not cooperate. This was an opportunity for Leah to gain favor with her husband. Leah could have children and she brought forth a succession of babies, but Jacob's feelings towards her remained the same. He was tricked into marrying her but would not be tricked into loving her. No doubt a mix of jealousy, anger, resentment and misery dwelled in that home. Further complicating matters, two handmaidens were brought in to be with Jacob and they bore more children. Leah hoped her life would improve when she began having children, but instead it only seemed to get worse.

Enough is Enough!

Leah's life was a sea of sadness, turmoil and disappointment and I believe she got to the point where she said enough is enough! Enough of the chaos, enough of the jealousy, enough of the back-biting and hatred, it must cease.

Enough! Many of you today need to get to the place where you put our foot down and say enough is enough! We have entertained mess, pettiness, drama and jealousy for far too long. It pains me to see people wasting time in petty church disputes and drawn out relationship games when there is a dying world outside our doors. There is so much to be done in the Kingdom! How dare we waste time with petty nonsense!

Where are those who will say enough is enough? Enough gossip, enough jealousy, enough being so consumed with busyness that we fail to see the plan of God upon our lives. Enough being paralyzed by fear and entangled with unforgiveness, enough running like Jonah and telling God what we will and will not do. Enough is enough! You must get to the place where you draw the line and out right refuse to be entangled, held back and bound any longer.

Leah's tent likely looked more like a war zone than a family home. Her friends and loved one treated her like the enemy. Walls of jealousy, division and resentment stood like partitions in her home. What a life of misery! This was not the life Leah hoped for. She too had hopes and desires, but her dreams of happiness seemed to amount to nothing. No matter how hard she tried her husband loved another woman. Leah faced discouragement daily and likely felt like giving up on life completely.

Something had to give. Something had to change. Leah birthed three children by Jacob. Yet, when she was pregnant with her fourth I believe Leah experienced a life changing shift.

The Red Tent

I believe that Leah rose from Jacob's tent as she was full term with her fourth child. I imagine she felt the signs of labor and knew it was time. In those days women went to a special tent to give birth. They went to a place called the red tent.

I can see Leah making her way to the red tent. As she pressed her way in her ninth month of gestation, something was happening on the inside of her. Leah had given birth before, this was her fourth baby. Leah was used to labor, she had already birthed three babies, but I imagine this one was different.

As Leah moved towards the red tent, the elder mothers of the village were already there making preparation for her arrival. They knew well the process of childbirth. They hummed a familiar tune as they awaited Leah's arrival. They knew Leah's time was drawing near and saw the tell-tale signs of a woman nearing her time of delivery days prior.

Leah's belly had dropped low so that even walking became difficult. Frequent pauses between steps were needed. Leah had resolved to using one of Jacob's staffs, she used it as a support, a walking stick and with it journeyed onward towards the red tent. There was no donkey to carry her to the red tent, but the elder mothers knew well the benefit of that uphill climb towards the red tent. Many a woman had crumpled mid-journey and delivered screaming babies through screams of their own, right there on the side of the hill.

As Leah made it to the red tent, I can see the elder mothers forming a circle of strength around her, ready to brace and support Leah. One especially old woman was already humming, low throaty soothing songs to help ease the mind and fears of all. The other women were silent. They waited for God and nature to take its course and thrust Leah into the familiar throes of labor. Time passed. A mother wiped Leah's brow and offered cool sips of water. Leah bent at the waist with each contraction. She was doing her best to stand and walk within the confines of the red tent, each step becoming increasingly difficult. As the all too familiar pain intensified, with her fourth child, Leah began to bear down and push. A birthing stool was placed beneath her to aid the process.

Now outside the tent Jacob and the people of the village were likely waiting for word of a successful delivery. I believe the villagers were used to the sounds of the birth tent. There were no epidurals in Leah's day. No drugs to ease the pain. So, it was commonplace for cries of agony and suffering to be heard emanating from the tent.

Yes, this labor was greatly different. God had a plan that was unfolding right there in the red tent. As Leah pushed and pushed in childbirth, something happened. As that fourth baby came forth, a new sound started emanating from that tent. A sound unlike any they had heard from Leah in the past. It was not the usual cries of agony and pain. See this was the sound of a woman who had been delivered. Leah's fourth child was called Judah and when Leah birthed Judah, she birthed her praise. The very name Judah means "praise." At that moment her name was changed from Leah meaning misery, to Judah's mother meaning the mother of praise.

Judah means praise! Some would say that Leah delivered Judah, but I believe that Judah delivered Leah. It was praise that broke her out of that place of misery and into the restoration power of God. Psalm 22:3 tells us that God inhabits the praises of His people. So, as that tent began to fill with newly born praise, it simultaneously filled with the presence of the Lord. Leah moved from dwelling in a tent of depression, turmoil and misery to a place filled with glorious praise and the presence of God. As Leah birthed her praise, she was delivered and transformed.

However, this great transition was not only for Leah, but also for those around her. Likewise, your praise isn't just for you. Leah's praise emanated out of the red tent and throughout the village transforming the atmosphere of the entire camp.

Praise brings a refreshing into the spirit and the soul. When you give thanks and have an attitude of praise, times of refreshing will come upon you. It is no coincidence that the Bible refers to the sacrifice of praise and the sacrifice of thanksgiving. I believe that is alluding to times when you very well may find yourself in a weak state where rendering praise to God does not flow as readily. Sometimes we have to press through some things in order to get into a place of praise and thanksgiving. You must never lose sight of the fact that offering the sacrifice of praise and thanksgiving, even in distressing circumstances, will help you to find a reservoir of God's strength and grace. Often times, when it is most difficult to offer the sacrifice of praise and thanksgiving, is when you need to do it the most. Though you may not feel like it, praise must not be conditional or about a feeling. The Lord has called you to give thanks at all times, not only when you feel like it.

David declared, "I will bless the Lord at all times, His praise shall continually be in my mouth" (Psalm 34:1 NKJV).

Christina M. Whitaker

Death Can't Have My Hope

No matter what you are facing and how dismal or discouraging the situation may seem you cannot allow your hope to die. You must get to a place where you refuse to hand over your hope and your faith. Never stop believing, never stop trusting and never stop hoping. Hope and faith in God are sure anchors that will keep you from drifting into discouragement when navigating the storms of life. Though you may be surrounded by desolation and death, you must choose to live. Cling to hope and refuse to let go.

The choice is yours. You can choose to embrace hope and live as an overcomer, or you can embrace death and live as a victim. When discouragement sets in it is easy to spiral into a place of hopelessness. It is not easy to keep hoping and standing on the promises. Sometimes believing that your dream will never happen is much easier than believing that it will. Ultimately, you cannot allow delay and discouragement to rob you of your hopes and dreams. Hold fast! Hold on and stand in faith. Refuse to give up. Look to God for strength and direction. Allow Him to renew your hope. You may face challenges, but life is still full of hope and opportunity. When challenges come, allow that challenge to make you stronger rather than defeat you.

Once you make the choice to live and to not die, then you must find the strength and the power to live. That power only comes from God. The psalmist understood this. He made a choice to live. "I will not die but live, and will proclaim what the Lord has done," (Psalm 118:17). When we choose to live and refuse to give up, by the power of God, our entire lives become a testimony and a proclamation of the goodness of God.

Choose life! How do we do this? Agree with God's Word and what He has spoken concerning your life. Refuse to agree with negative circumstances. Refuse to succumb to the agony of delay and defeat. Keep trying, keep hoping, keep believing. Let your actions reflect life, rather than hopelessness and death.

Some years ago I started writing a book, because things did not progress the way I desired I gave up. Completely stopped writing for a number of years. I allowed death and defeat to steal my hope and temporarily steal the promise

I knew God had spoken to me. I gave up for a season, and that is what happens with many of us. Don't allow your dreams to die. You must not. What is it that you long to accomplish? What is it that burns in your heart? It doesn't matter if obstacles stand in your way. The best stand you can take is a stand in faith upon God's Word. Choose life each and every day. Speak life to your situation and refuse to give up hope.

Chapter 8: Focus Forward

One chilly November night, my husband was away traveling. Our daughters and I were nestled snuggly in our beds. Around two a.m. I woke up and reached to the cluttered nightstand for my glasses. Half-awake, my hand groped around for several seconds trying to locate my precious glasses. Precious is an understatement. My vision without glasses is a far cry from 20/20 vision. When I open my eyes each morning, securing my glasses on my face is the first thing I do. I need them in order to get out of bed, navigate to the restroom and babies' room, and even to see the flashing clock perched no less than three feet away on our nightstand. A small wave of panic washed over me as I reached again for my beloved glasses. I jokingly refer to my glasses as "my eyes," because without them I truly cannot see.

Satisfied that the glasses were not on the nightstand, I carefully rolled out of bed and onto the floor starting a hands and knees two a.m. search-and-rescue mission, being oh so careful not to crush them. I searched under the bed, around the room, in the bathroom, everywhere I imagined they could be. I wondered if my five year old, Olivia, had secretly taken them to adorn one of her baby dolls while playing dress-up or some other make believe game. I crawled down the dark hallway to her room being careful to avoid the stairwell and searched through her army of animals and toys. It was to no avail. My glasses were nowhere to be found. I had been searching for almost an hour when fear and dread welled up in my heart. My stomach churned. I could not see! The world around me was a blurry mess!

I wondered if I would have to remain in the house with our two children until my husband returned home the following night. There was no way I could leave the house, cook meals, or do so many of the things necessary to care for the girls. I wondered if I'd even be able to make it down our steep flight of stairs with the baby! I would not be able to drive. Olivia would have to miss school. All of these thoughts flooded my mind as I wracked my brain for where my vision, "my eyes" could be? I considered waking Olivia to help me search, but it was now three a.m. and desperate as I was, I resolved to find them alone and let her sleep. I wracked my brain one final time and gave the room another desperate sweep looking in the baby's crib and absolutely everywhere! I considered calling my husband, but I knew he would worry and try to find a way home.

In a last ditch effort I moved our king-sized bed away from the wall and to my amazement and utter relief, there were my glasses. I must have fallen asleep with the glasses on and during the night they slipped down the tiny space between the mattress and headboard and fell behind the bed. I was so thankful. I thanked God repeatedly as relief washed over me.

Discovering Your Path

I knew there was a message, something to be gained from that experience. Sure, sleeping in your glasses is to be avoided at all costs, but I am referring to a different type of message. I believe that many in the world today are going through life without sufficient vision.

Proverbs 29:18 KJV says, "Where there is no vision, the people perish: but he that keepeth the law, happy is he." The NKJV says, "Where there is no revelation, the people perish." The term vision in these texts can refer to revelation or insight, which are necessary for us to successfully navigate our path in life. When people lack revelation, insight and awareness of their purpose: dreams and destinies are at risk of perishing.

Without vision it is nearly impossible to reach your destination or destiny.

God wants to enlighten you to His plans and purposes for your life. It is not His will that you grope around blindly, stumbling aimlessly through life. There is a purpose for your life and the promises of God for your life are sure, but you must be able to hear and discern God's leading concerning His vision for your life. It is through vision that you are given a revelation of where God desires to lead you. Without vision, there is great risk of wandering, making unnecessary wrong-turns in life, and even completely straying from the path and promises God has predestined for your life. Without vision it is nearly impossible to reach your destination or destiny.

When you have a revelation of who you are, who God is, and what He has called you to do in the earth you are armed for success!

> Paul said it masterfully when he prayed for the Church of Ephesus, "The eyes of your understanding being enlightened; that ye may know what is the hope of his calling, and what the riches of the glory of his inheritance in the saints, And what is the exceeding greatness of His power to us-ward who believe, according to the working of His mighty power," (Ephesians 1:18-19 KJV).

When God opens the eyes of your understanding, you are given a clearer view of your purpose and calling. An understanding of who you are must be awakened. To operate based on what you think God has called you to do, is not enough. Having clear vision, insight and understanding is necessary to successfully remain on and navigate your path. Even if you have a clear idea of God's purpose and destiny for your life, I believe you can still benefit from fresh revelation and vision. Ask God to clarify and sharpen your vision. Ask Him to reveal His plans and purposes for your life. Ask Him to give you a clear vision for today, tomorrow and beyond.

Just Ask

Jeremiah 33:3 is a favorite Scripture and one full of insight and direction for those seeking to discover their purpose and direction. "Call unto Me and I will answer you and show you great and mighty things that you know not," (Jeremiah 33:3). The Lord instructs you to ask when you desire to know something that has not yet been revealed. He goes on to say that when you call Him, that He will answer you and reveal things which you do not know.

Take a sure stand upon this promise. Do not be satisfied with not knowing your purpose and direction in life. Ask God and expect Him to answer you. He may not reveal the answer immediately, but in time it will be revealed.

I have encountered many people who spend years desperately trying to discover who they are and why they are here, what their purpose is in life and how to progress down the right path. Ephesians 1:18 provides a solution for this very quandary. It is God's will for you to come into a progressive place of understanding and awareness of your purpose. If you have never prayed Ephesians 1:18 over your life, business, family and ministry, I encourage you to do so today and continue on a regular basis.

Personal Prayer

Lord, I pray for the eyes of my understanding to be opened and enlightened, so that I will know the hope of your calling for my life. I want to know your plans and purposes for my life Reveal the hidden things and cause light to shine upon my path. Give me a revelation of your glory, power and greatness for me. Refresh my vision and lead me in the path of Your plans and promises for my life. In Jesus Name, Amen!

Your Focus is Key

In pursuing the plans of God for your life and journeying through life's peaks, valleys and every place in-between, your focus is key. Have you ever found yourself driving through your city, which you may drive through daily, and before you know it you have missed your turn or passed your exit? There have been times when I have to do a U-turn, because I completely passed my destination. We must remain focused even when we think we know where God is taking us. Do not become distracted by what is going on around you or by what is happening to you. Your focus should be fixed on God and His Word and the destination He has set before you.

Standing on the Promises

Speaking of eyes, have you ever been to an optometrist? Usually when you first look through the examination machine the letters and images appear blurry and difficult to read, especially for me. The optometrist may make a few adjustments and suddenly what was once blurry comes into focus. The letters and images were clearly there all along, but you could not clearly perceive it when you saw it initially. It can be quite similar with the details of your life. You know that you have a purpose and destiny, but at present they may appear unclear, foggy, blurred and even hidden. At this point in your life your destiny may not have come into clear focus, but that does not mean that you do not have a destiny and purpose. You most certainly do. There are great promises assigned to your life and focusing on God will keep you on the path of reaping the rewards He has for your life.

Focus on God

Consider Peter in Matthew 14, who was able to do the impossible and walk on water, when his eyes were fixed on Jesus. Yet, as soon as he allowed his vision to take in his surroundings, and he saw the tempestuous storm swirling around him he became fearful, doubted and started to sink. He went from walking on water to sinking just that quickly when his focus waned. It is important to note that when Peter was focused on Jesus, his faith was strong and he was going forward even in a seemingly impossible situation. He advanced with great success in the midst of impossibility. However, when he took his eyes of the Lord, and his focused shifted to the troubles surrounding him, doubt crept in swiftly and caused him to stumble.

Circumstances speak, but God spoke first, and He has the final say!

Your focus on God is a significant key in your success. You must remain focus on what God has spoken concerning your life, even when it seems to be impossible. Your faith must remain in God. In essence that is the heart of standing on the promises, simply take a firm stance on what God has spoken and refuse to be moved by the winds and storms of life, no matter what is going on around you. When you take a determined stand and refuse to shift your focus from the surety of God's Word, you close the door to doubt and fear. Circumstances speak, but God spoke first, and He has the final say!

> "Lord, if it's you," Peter replied, "Tell me to come to you on the water." "Come," he said. Then Peter got down out of the boat, walked on the water and came toward Jesus, but when he saw the wind, he was afraid and, beginning to sink, cried out, "Lord, save me!" Immediately Jesus reached out his hand and caught him. "You of little faith," he said, "why did you doubt?" (Matthew 14:28-31 NIV).

Peter was a brave fellow. The other disciples were stuck to their seats in the safety of the boat, but Peter had a measure of curious faith that welled up within him. When Jesus said "come" and encouraged Peter to step out on the water, Peter obeyed and suddenly he was walking out a miracle. Peter stepped onto the infallible truth of God's Word. God's Word is infallible, it cannot fail. When Jesus said, "come," Peter did not step out onto the water, he stepped out on the Word issued from God, which cannot fail. That is critical to note. Peter did not step out onto the water; he stepped out on the infallible Word of God. The place where Peter planted his foot was a sure place and an eternal place. He stepped out onto the Word of God.

The other disciples were stuck to their seats in the safety of the boat, but Peter had a measure of curious faith that welled up within him.

Peter utilized two significant keys: faith and obedience. Likewise, when God speaks to your heart and gives you an instruction, if you step out in obedience to Him, your pathway is sure. You will not fall or fail as long as you are walking in obedience to His will, because God's Word is incapable of failure. Now, there are times when you may get ahead of Him or lag behind Him. Can you see that now? Peter stood in the midst of the sea on top of the word "come," that was spoken by Jesus, but if Peter had taken several steps to the right or left, he could have stepped outside of the grace and direction of that word. Sometimes that is precisely what we do. The Lord says "go" and we take off and never look back. We never listen for another piece of instruction from the Lord, and we step right outside of the realm of grace extended for that word.

You must do as Peter initially did, step out in faith and remained focused. When focusing on God, you must remain focused on God. That may seem overly simple, but it is deeply important. Your focus must remain on God and His Word. It does not matter if there is a storm raging around you. It does not matter what the economy is doing or what your bank account has or lacks, Jesus said, "come," and that is the word of truth you must step out on in complete faith. As long as Peter was focused on Jesus, he walked atop the water, but as soon as he shifted his focus to his surroundings, doubt crept in and his surroundings began to overtake him. Jesus chastised him after coming to his rescue saying," You of little faith," he said, "why did you doubt?"

Lot's Wife Syndrome

Have you ever seen someone trying to go forward, but they cannot seem to do so, because their focus is on what's behind them? Genesis 19 shares the account of Lot and his family. The wicked conditions and the deafening cries of the victims in Sodom and Gomorrah had risen before God, and angels were dispatched to issue God's judgment and destroy the cities. Lot was a recipient of God's grace. He and his family were given an opportunity to exit the city before the death decree was carried out. Many have heard of Lot's wife, she is known simply as "Lot's wife" or "the one who looked back." She was given a ticket out of town, a pass granting her escape from the impending destruction. She and her family were given one instruction, "go and do not look back." You probably already know the outcome of this unfortunate account. Lot's wife did look back and her life came to a screeching halt as she was changed into a pillar of salt in that very place (Genesis 19:26). She looked back, and it cost her everything.

There is much to be learned from the fate of Lot's wife. What she did is not that uncommon. Many find themselves in the throes of transition and change, moving from one place to another, and they experience a pull from their past or a strong desire to return to the familiar. Many end up looking back and even yearning to go back to that familiar place. Even when the place God is taking you to is a place of greater promotion and blessing, there may be a pull from the familiarity of where you have been that beckons you relentlessly. It seems irrational to think someone would give up greatness before them to wallow in the mud of their past, but it happens all the time. Many find that their past is a place of comfort, pleasure and familiarity. They know it, even if it is undesirable or detrimental. Do not live your life parked in neutral or going in reverse, your destiny and future are ahead of you, not behind you.

At times change can be intensely difficult. It may seem comforting to reminisce and allow your thoughts to frolic with the past, but this can bring a destructive end as we saw with Lot's wife.

The Past

The past is just that, it is the past. Yet, many find themselves stuck in that very place with an inability to successfully advance. Why? What is it about the past that woos people and lures them even when their heart is set on moving forward? There are times when you must sever ties with people, businesses and relationships. In order to fully embrace your future you must let go of your past. Do not be afraid to sever such ties. It may seem cruel, but continuing to hold on to the past will prevent you from moving forward into the new.

Some people find themselves going backwards, taking one step forward and two steps back as the cliché' goes. Their intentions are admirable, hopes and dreams are present, and yet they find themselves returning to the very people, places and events of their past even when those things were unproductive or even hurtful. It is a vicious cycle that should be broken in order to effectively move forward. If Lot's wife had quickly severed ties with Sodom and Gomorrah, I believe she would have been able to successfully

Standing on the Promises

evacuate the city, and move on to the new place God had graced them to enter. When Lot's wife attempted to evacuate the city, her feet were moving forward, but her heart and mind were still roaming about in Sodom and Gomorrah.

Looking Back Can Be Deadly

I worked as a psychiatric nurse for ten years, and I encountered many people with heart rending stories. I want to tell you about one lady. Her name and certain details of her story have been altered to protect her identity. Let's call her Amy. Amy was in the throes of a twelve year cycle of abuse. Amy had been involved with a man for twelve years or more, no children, but much pain, agony and heartache filled their troubled relationship. The fellow she was dangerously intertwined with treated her cruelly. He prided himself on being a tyrant. He was controlling, domineering and treated Amy more like an animal than a human. It was no surprise to see Amy with bruises, bandages and broken bones.

On one occasion, the fellow walked in on Amy talking and laughing with a girlfriend on the phone and he launched into a violent fit of rage. Amy later recounted that in a jealous rage he tore pictures from the wall and hurled them at her. He broke a vase over her head, hit her relentlessly with a statue that usually rested on the coffee table and left her lying in a pool of her own blood.

Over the years there were numerous emergency room visits for Amy. The police were called countless times to come to her aid. This dear woman was taken away to safety, given housing and a fresh start time after time. Counselors, police officers, psychiatric staff, spiritual leaders and advocates admonished her to take action and press charges. They begged her to move forward with her life. The fellow served short stents in jail, but whenever he got out, Amy found her way back to him. That was interesting. He did not have to go looking for Amy. When he got out of jail each time, Amy knew it and sought him out.

Time after time she nodded her swollen head, thankful for the care and concern others offered. Time after time the advice appeared to sink in. She even lived in a safe house for a number of months on one occasion. Eventually the voices from her past outweighed the voices beckoning her forward and she retreated back to the prison of turmoil and abuse. Fear paralyzed her from moving forward and the familiar called to her. I really believe Amy wanted to get away from him, but despite all of the interventions and help she never did. She resolved to remain with her lover. Somehow the word "lover" does little to describe their bitter relationship.

Years after I had lost contact with Amy, I learned of her dreaded account while watching the evening News. I wished it were not so. As the story goes, for two years Amy lived in a safe house, walking out the fresh start that had filled her dreams. Amy seemed to have succeeded in moving forward and picking up the pieces of her battered life. She moved to another city, found a decent job and the scars of her past were beginning to heal. However, one night, she went back. She returned to that savage relationship, for the last time. Her lover greeted her at the door with the sting of a backhand and an onslaught of degrading accusations. A tussle ensued. He threatened to kill her for leaving him. He violently promised that she would never leave him again. His hands gripped her throat as he sought to squeeze the life from her frail body. In a burst of rage he threw her against the wall. Amy scrambled to the bedroom, and locked the door. Her assailant banged and kicked at the door repeatedly, trying relentlessly to break it down. Amy was tired of fighting and angry at herself for returning to that prison of pain. In an act of hopeless desperation, Amy pulled out a gun, the gun that always rested in a box beneath her lover's bed. The same gun he had used over the years to threaten her life. The same gun he brutally beat her with in years past, causing a river of blood to journey down her face. Amy picked up that gun and shot herself. There on the bedroom floor she ended the nightmarish cycle of abuse and torment.

Did her life have to end that way? I say no, certainly not. Amy deserved so much more, and she deserved none of the pain, torment and mistreatment that filed her life. I believe if Amy had severed that deep familiar connection to her past, she would have been able to move forward into her future. This is a tragic account, but one that needs to be shared. The pull of your past can be deadly, resulting in destruction, spiritual death or even forfeiture of the plan of God for your life.

It may not be abuse and pain in your past. It could be a job that you left years ago, a church, a relationship or even a business venture. Yet, you find yourself thinking about it, hurt about it, yearning for it and maybe even trying to find ways to return to that place of satisfaction if even for a moment.

There are times when it is necessary to make a clean break with certain people and even relationships that are unhealthy. Do not be afraid to let go of the past. Many people carry terribly hurtful memories with them. Let go of past hurts and tormenting memories. Choosing to let go is one of the most liberating things you can do. Choose to let go of the fear, hurt and pain. When you let go you are freed to move forward into your future. Never allow your past to hold you captive. Throughout the Bible we see God leading people forward. That is how God operates, by taking you forward. At times you may enter a season of waiting, but your future is in front of you, not behind you. If there are hurtful experiences in your past that continue to torment you and great disappointments that refuse to let you go, pray this prayer with me. Let's believe God for your victory over the past.

Choosing to let go is one of the most liberating things you can do.

Personal Prayer

Dear God. Thank You for being my refuge and strength. Thank You for being my help and protector. I know that You will never leave me or forsake me and even in difficult times you were there all along. Now I ask You to show Yourself strong and mighty in my life as my Deliverer. Deliver me from the pull of my past and sever all unhealthy connections with my past. Heal every wound from past hurts and abuses. Help me to go forward once and for all. Right now I release everyone who has hurt me in the past and I forgive them. I go forward free, without the pain of my past. Help me to embrace all that you have destined for me. In Jesus Name, Amen.

Chapter 9: Delight in Him

There is a book called Ezra in the Bible. There we discover much about Ezra the notable scribe. We learn that God's hand of grace, favor and blessing was upon Ezra and all he set his heart to do because of his devotion to knowing, studying and obeying God's Word. That is well worth reiterating, because this is an area where many miss the mark. Many hear the Word of God taught on Sunday mornings and even try diligently to walk in the will of God, but fall short when it comes to taking the initiative to read and store God's Word in their hearts. God's hand of grace, favor and blessing was upon Ezra and all he set his heart to do because of his devotion to knowing, studying and obeying God's Law.

> "On the first day of the first month he came to Jerusalem, according to the good hand of his God upon him. For Ezra prepared his heart to seek the Law of the Lord, and to do it, and to teach statutes and ordinances in Israel." (Ezra 7:9-10 NIV).

Ezra was a great Scribe and therefore, his life was centered on recording, studying and teaching God's Law. Ezra knew God's Law and he spent abundant time therein. I believe it is safe to say that Ezra delighted in God.

Delighting in God Releases Blessings

When you delight in God and His Word you become a recipient of wonderful blessings from God. Great reward is promised to those who delight in God and His Word.

"Blessed is the man that walketh not in the counsel of the ungodly, nor standeth in the way of sinners, nor sitteth in the seat of the scornful. But his delight is in the law of the Lord; and in his law doth he meditate day and night. And he shall be like a tree planted by the rivers of water, that bringeth forth his fruit in his season; his leaf also shall not wither; and whatsoever he doeth shall prosper," (Psalm 1:1-3 KJV).

When you spend time delving into the Word of God consistently, you can expect to have a solid foundation and a strong root system. Then you will be like the Psalm 1 tree planted by the rivers of water. You will grow and flourish. When you are rooted and grounded in the Word of God you will drink deeply from His truth and you shall not be a weak or withering tree. Your branches and leaves will be strong, a testament of the life giving power of God's Word. You will grow and flourish and your plans will grow and prosper, because you have purposed it in your heart to study and delight in the Word of God. When your delight is in the Lord you will spend time meditating on His Word day and night (Psalm 1:2).

When you are rooted and grounded in the Word of God you will drink deeply from His truth and you shall not be a weak or withering tree.

The latter portion of Psalm 1:3 reveals another blessing extended to those who delight in God and His Word: whatever you do will prosper. What a glorious promise! When you delight in the Lord and in His Word and spend time studying and meditating therein, you will have good success and everything that you do shall prosper. That is an incredible promise. Many in the body of Christ have overlooked this opportunity for blessing. Yet, the Word of God is sure. When you delight in God, He will make your way sure, He will prosper you and give you good success. If your pathway has been troubled or uncertain, begin to delight in God and His Word. Study and meditate on His Word. He will make your way sure and successful.

Standing on the Promises

Nehemiah spoke these words, "O Lord, please hear my prayer! Listen to the prayers of those of us who delight in honoring you. Please grant me success today by making the king give favor to me." Nehemiah and his servants delighted in revering and honoring God, therefore they expected God's grace, favor and blessing to be extended unto them (Nehemiah 1:11 NLT).

Did you realize that it is Biblical to pray for success and favor? Nehemiah and his team prayed for success prior to and throughout their building project. They tapped into unusual favor and success in their endeavors, quite possibly the result of purposing in their hearts to delight in God and come before Him in prayer. When you delight in God and His Word you should expect to reap blessings of favor and success. It is time to raise your level of expectation.

Learning to Delight

The word delight is most frequently expressed in the Bible by the Hebrew word hapes or chaphets, which can mean "to bend" or "to incline to." Those who delight and take pleasure in God and His Word bend their existence toward Him. That is an important key in the life of every believer. Far too often people live their lives leaning to their own understanding and only drawing near to God during times of need or trouble. God desires that you delight in Him and incline yourself to Him at all times, not only when trouble arises.

James 4:8 tells us that when we draw near to God, He responds and draws near to us. You should spend time drawing near to God daily. Ways of drawing near to God include, but are not limited to prayer, fasting, time with the Lord, reading the Bible and worship. To come to God only when you need something grossly misses the fullness of the relationship God created you to have with Him.

Draw near to God and make time and room for Him in your life. However, it does not stop there. To delight in Him carries a much deeper meaning. As you seek to delight in God there should be a bending, yielding and inclining to Him in all areas of your life. At its origin, to "delight in," from the Hebrew word chaphets, means to bend towards something and incline to it. This moves beyond drawing near. This indicates a yearning, a longing and a great desire to reach the Lord, encounter Him and experience His presence.

Delighting in the Master

This reminds me of the woman with the issue of blood (Luke 8:43). The woman had been sick with a bleeding disorder for twelve long years. She had seen numerous doctors and spent all her money seeking a cure, but to no avail. When Jesus came to town she was determined to reach Him. She was desperate. There was a deep longing and knowing within her that drove her onward, though she was supposed to stay away from others because of the nature of her infirmity. She had to get close. Sure, there were throngs of people pressed in around Him, but this woman would not be denied. She delighted in Him, she drew near and her heart was bent towards Him. She pressed through the painful circumstances of her own existence and reached for Him with all her might. She reached Him and though she was considered unclean, she touched the hem of His garments. Immediately, she was restored and made whole. When you delight in the Lord, your heart will bend towards Him in total honor and adoration. You will desire more of Him and seek after Him with great longing and yearning.

To delight in Him denotes a progression, it is when you move beyond the perimeter (outer courts), and pursue Him with great passion, desperation and hunger. When you delight in God, you bend your entire existence to Him. "At the name of Jesus, every knee should bow, in heaven and on earth and under the earth" (Philippians 2:10). Bow to Him and lay your burdens and cares at His feet. Delight in His presence and yearn for more of Him. When you truly delight in God and His Word out of a heart of love and devotion you will lovingly bend away from the world, and incline yourself ever closer to the Lord.

Standing on the Promises

When you delight in Him you will "bend" or "lean" towards God. This is a posture of trust and dependence on God that you should take. You are called to stand on the promises and lean eternally on His everlasting arms.

"Trust in the Lord with all thine heart, and lean not unto thine own understanding. In all thy ways acknowledge Him and He shall direct thy paths," (Proverbs 3:5-6 KJV). "Trust in the Lord with all your heart." Not half your heart, all your heart. To trust God completely means that you must be willing to let go, and allow God to take the reins of your life. Allow Him to lead as you follow.

We must trust God enough to let go, relinquish control and welcome God's hand in your life. To trust Him with all your heart means just that, all of your heart, no matter what the situation looks like or feels like. Rest assured that God is in control. He shall see you through every situation.

To trust God completely means that you must be willing to let go, and allow God to take the reins of your life.

"And lean not unto thine own understanding." How often do you try to figure things out on your own instead of seeking God for direction? This passage explains that you should not lean or rely on your own understanding, instead you should lean and depend fully on God. God wants to give you wisdom, direction and strategy for success and advancement, but you can miss that if you are leaning solely on your intelligence and strength.

"In all thy ways acknowledge Him." You must know and believe that God is God, and because He is God, nothing is impossible for Him. He holds the answers to every mystery of life and the answers to your every situation. You must acknowledge His glory, power and wisdom. Realize that without Him, you are nothing and it is futile to try and live this life without Him. Enthrone Him in His proper place in your life, acknowledging who He is at all times. When you do this, God is increased in your life.

"And He shall direct thy paths." When you diligently implement these steps there is a promise that you will lay hold of, the Lord will direct your paths. You will not have to worry about which way to go, which offer to take or when to go, because God will direct your every step and decision. What an awesome promise to have. To know that God is concerned about even the tiniest details of your life and wants to lead you down the path of success and blessing.

Chapter 10: Be Ready When Opportunity Knocks

When opportunity comes knocking at your door, no matter what phase of life you are in, it behooves you to be ready. At the sound of the knock is not the time to begin preparing for the opportunity at your door. Preparation should be done in advance. The failure to adequately prepare can prove to be delaying or even detrimental to your success and progress.

Know When Your Time Has Arrived

In September 2006 I woke in the middle of the night with bad stomach pains. I was thirty-seven weeks into my first pregnancy and I began to wonder if "this was it." I called Tony. He was working third shift an hour away. I advised him to stay by the phone. By the time I got out of the shower the contractions were five to six minutes apart, consistent and strong. My husband came racing home and found me doubled over in pain. The pain was so intense, our midwife urged us to hurry to the hospital.

When we left the house the contractions were already two to three minutes apart. My husband ran around frantically throwing bags into the car, looking for keys, and grabbing a few final items. He jumped in the car and started to back out of the driveway, realizing that I was still standing on the front porch. He leapt out of the car and gingerly hurried me down the driveway and into the passenger seat. I strapped on my seatbelt between "hee-hee-hoos" and we sped off into the night.

It was two a.m. and most people were slumbering peacefully in their beds, I on the other hand was sweating profusely and desperately trying to remember absolutely anything I had learned in Lamaze class. The contractions were consistently two to three minutes apart and increasingly painful. Halfway to the hospital, Tony gasped and slapped the steering wheel.

"I have something to tell you," my husband said quietly.

Now granted this was not the time for telling me much of anything but I glanced in his direction waiting to hear what he had to say. He paused for what seemed like an eternity, and then hurriedly blurted out in a single breath, "I brought the camera to take pictures, but forgot to get a memory card for the camera, so we won't be able to take any pictures of the labor and delivery. I know you said pack it but I forgot."

I believe razor sharp darts shot from my eyes as my head swerved around in his direction. Before I could open my mouth, another contraction gripped me and I resulted in a series of "hee-hee-YOU's!"

"There's a Walmart right here. I can run in really fast and get it, and then get you to the hospital," he offered apologetically.

Without thinking I shook my head in agreement and loosened my grip on the dashboard as the contraction began to ease. Tony sped through the Walmart parking lot, onto the sidewalk, and parked right in the doorway to our local Walmart. A few wide-eyed late night employees dove out of the way as Tony shouted, "My wife's having a baby right now" and ran through the front doors into Walmart.

I, on the other hand, was in far too much pain to care that our car was sitting on the sidewalk in the entranceway to a Walmart. A horrifying thought entered my mind, *What if I have this baby in the Walmart parking lot?* I started praying furiously, *Lord please, please don't let our baby be born in a Walmart parking lot*! I could envision the newspaper headlines: "Husband forgets camera and wife has baby at Walmart!"

In less than five minutes Tony came running out with a tiny bag, waving it like a golden ticket. He dove into the car and we continued on our speeding journey to the hospital. Thankfully, we made it to the hospital in plenty of time and Olivia was not born at Walmart.

I could envision the newspaper headlines: "Husband forgets

camera and wife has baby at Walmart!"

It is critically important in life that we are prepared. Ezra in the Bible, prepared adequately and therefore he was found ready. When the Lord placed in his heart a desire to go and rebuild the wall in Jerusalem, he was ready. His lifestyle was one of preparation. We see from the book of Ezra that he was a man who communed with God, studied the Law and spent time in prayer and seeking the Lord. Ezra was a notable scribe, therefore, we can safely assume that he spent long hours studying and recording the Law. When the opportunity arose his times of study and preparation ensured that he was adequately prepared to lead and move the people forward efficiently. His mission was great. He led a caravan of people nine hundred miles by foot and headed up a major architectural project, the rebuilding of Jerusalem's walls and gates.

A Parable of Readiness

Consider the parable of the ten virgins in Matthew 25. In this story, there were ten virgins who took their lamps and went out to meet the bridegroom. Five of the virgins were foolish and five were wise. The foolish ones were labeled foolish, because they took their lamps with them but failed to take any oil. However, the wise virgins took oil in jars with their lamps. The bridegroom appeared at midnight, a time when all of the virgins were sleeping. All of the virgins got up and trimmed their lamps. The foolish virgins did not have enough oil and were unprepared for the bridegrooms visit. They asked the wise ones for some of their oil, but were refused, because the wise did not have enough for both of them. The foolish virgins rushed off to get oil. The bridegroom arrived while they were trying to gather oil and prepare.

The wise virgins were ready and went in with the bridegroom to the wedding banquet. Once they were inside the door was closed. Sometime later, the foolish virgins returned and asked that the door be opened, but it was too late. This is critically important. The door was closed. It was too late. The foolish virgins were unprepared and therefore missed their window of opportunity. The wise virgins were ready for the bridegroom's appearance, because they had made necessary preparations and gathered their oil ahead of time.

A lifestyle of readiness will help ensure that you do not miss opportunities, open doors, times of promotion, advancement and more. Most of all being "ready" and watchful will help ensure that you do not miss God.

The five wise virgins were watchmen. There is a call for the Body of Christ to awaken from slumber and arise in the earth. Segments of the Church throughout the world have been awakening and arising, but there is a need for the entire body of believers to arise throughout the earth, and take a stand for righteousness and truth. You must be alert and awake in order to watch and be vigilant. Too many are in a state of spiritual slumber oblivious to the voice of God and the call upon their lives, clinging to their beds of comfort and complacency. Answer the call of prayer will strategically position you to receive insight and revelation from the Lord. This is the essence of watching, you are positioned to hear, see, and receive that which the Lord has for you. The wise virgins understood this. How sad for the foolish virgins. They missed out on what they assumed was theirs. They assumed the bridegroom would be theirs automatically, though they had failed to prepare. They were sadly mistaken.

Be alert and watchful so that you do not miss anything that God has for you. Too many people get stuck in the rut of procrastination and the "I still have time" mindset. Many rely on that excuse, and use it to rationalize their reasons for delaying. Put the excuses to rest today and embrace God's desire for you to dwell in a state of readiness.

"No more excuses," is one of the greatest strategies we can employ! Are you known for making excuses and procrastinating? Make a decision to end the cycle of excuses and take deliberate steps of setting daily goals and accomplishing them consistently. Procrastination is a rut that can quickly progress into a ditch, a hole, and then a deep canyon. Do not allow procrastination and excuses to consume your dreams. Take authority and deliberate action. Set goals instead of making excuses. Make a decision to move forward and leave past failures behind you. Work diligently to be prepared when opportunities come your way.

"No more excuses," is one of the greatest strategies we can employ!

Check your lamp. Is there oil in your lamp? Are you prepared? There may be dreams gestating in your heart, but what are you actively doing to prepare for and move towards those goals. A great secret to success can be summed up in two simple words, be prepared. You do not have to be the smartest person, most talented or anointed, but adequate preparation will position you for success and advancement.

Pride is Not Preparedness

A high level of intelligence, skill or even anointing can lead some to self-ascend into a place of believing they do not need to prepare. This attitude can easily morph into pride. Pride can cause you to skip or abbreviate your season of preparation. This could prove detrimental to all involved. Consider a turkey. When cooking that plump fifteen pound turkey for your family to eat, would you cook it for only an hour, and then attempt to serve it for dinner? Hopefully not! The bird would still be raw and anyone who dared taste it could easily become dangerously sick. Why? The turkey was not yet ready, the process of preparing it not yet complete. Similarly, many people are in diverse stages of process and preparation. Your process may be lengthy just like the turkey. Your process may be hot, intense, and uncomfortable as some things are being burned away. There are times when God needs to refine our character, and remove those things that are not like God. Preparation is a process and yours may be different from everyone else's. Whatever your process looks like, you should not seek to circumvent or abbreviate your time of preparation. In so doing you stand the risk of endangering yourself and others, and the risk of failure is much greater.

Consider a young girl who dreams of becoming a concert pianist, but despite her dreams fails to attend classes, trainings, workshops and private lessons. She believes that her natural talent is enough and additional preparation and training is not needed. In her prideful thinking she circumvents much of her process and the avenues of preparation available to her. When the grand day of symphony auditions arrive, she will likely find herself grossly unprepared. Do not venture down that same path. Take every opportunity to be found ready. Preparation may seem tedious or even painful, but it is for your making and for your good! Do not rush your process! Let God have His perfect work in you (Philippians 1:6).

Preparation should be a part of your lifestyle, done consistently along the course of your journey. In many cases you cannot wait until the opportunity has been fully revealed before you start preparing. The failure to adequately prepare can be the result of pride or even fear. If this be the case, it must be dealt with, otherwise you could continuously hinder yourself from being prepared for the opportunities God has for you. Advantageous preparation is evidenced when you live a lifestyle of preparation and readying, therefore when opportunity knocks, you can open the door with confidence and satisfaction that you are adequately prepared for the opportunity at hand.

Chapter 11: The Fight of Your Life

Have you ever wondered why boxers and fighters are also called "contenders?" They enter the ring and face an opponent often of comparable weight and stature, and a match ensues. It is a test of wills, endurance and maneuvers, each trying to gain the upper hand and each trying to triumph over their opponent. They contend for the victory. Often the matches are intense tests of strategy and skill. Likewise, God has called each of us to contend in life. We must contend for the promises.

Many people find themselves in a place of wanting and waiting, hoping and believing for something that has yet to materialize. It could be a dream, a business venture, a vision, a witty invention, any number of things. There are times when your hopes and dreams may be great, but the fulfillment of such promises seems delayed. During these times of believing, hoping and waiting your focus and faith must remain strong. Ward off discouragement and despair by focusing on the promise gestating in your heart.

The time for taking a passive approach to the promises and plans of God is over! Contend for the victory in your life! Discover God's plans and purposes for your life and stand firm in your pursuit. It is easy to be blown off track by the winds of life, yet resolute faith is required. Actively and passionately pursue the promises of God for your life.

The time for taking a passive approach to the promises and plans of God is over!

Contend vs. Content

Have you grown content in life? Have you accepted how things are and believe that they cannot change? Do you lack the drive to pursue the fullness of God's will and purposes for your life? It could be that contentment has replaced your will to contend. To contend can mean to struggle, to wage war, to fight for, or to wrestle. On the other hand, content can mean to desire no more than what one has. A content mindset is the state of many in the world today. They have become satisfied, comfortable even complacent and lost their motivation and desire for more. Even though they know and understand that God has promised them more, their mindset of contentment says that what they have is enough. As it relates to the promises of God, you must have a mindset to contend for all God has promised you and not settle for anything less.

> So, Jacob was left alone, and a man wrestled with him till daybreak. When the man saw that he could not overpower him, he touched the socket of Jacob's hip so that his hip was wrenched as he wrestled with the man. Then the man said, "Let me go, for it is daybreak." But Jacob replied, "I will not let you go unless you bless me," (Genesis 32:24-26 NIV). This is a powerful stretch of Scripture.

There were great blessings and promises ordained for Jacob's life and lineage. God had released magnificent promises upon Jacob's grandfather, Abraham, and those promises were generational. Jacob was rightly positioned to inherit and receive the blessings of God. The name Jacob can mean trickster. Some would say that name suited Jacob considering he tricked his brother, Esau out of his birthright blessing.

However, there was a great destiny upon Jacob that was revealed in greater measure in Genesis 32. Jacob encountered a heavenly representative and began to contend with that angel. Jacob refused to let the angel go until he released blessing upon his life, and so the wrestling match ensued. When was the last time you dug in your heels and wrestled and fought for what you know God has promised you? Jacob contended and wrestled, he warred and stood his ground, and he refused to give up until the blessing was released. That too must be your stance. You may know that God has spoken a blessing concerning you, but what are you doing about it. Is it sitting neatly on a shelf like a dusty picture frame, or are you keeping that promise fresh in your mind and before your eyes, praying into it and calling it forth. There are great promises ordained for your life and lineage and sometimes you will have to contend in faith, prayer and fasting for the release of those blessings.

When was the last time you dug in your heels and wrestled and fought for what you know God has promised you?

Genesis 32 says that Jacob and the angel wrestled until daybreak. When daybreak came, the angel rewarded Jacob for contending. Not only did he receive a commanded blessing, but his name was also changed from Jacob (trickster) to Israel (God's chosen). Jacob's contending showed his faith and refusal to give up on what God had destined for his life and lineage. You too should have a heart to hold on to and contend, through prayer, fasting and a firm stance upon God's promises for all that He has promised you and your lineage.

Jude 1:3 tells us to earnestly contend for the faith. Earnestly contend is our God given instruction. Someone who earnestly contends is committed and passionate about what they are pursuing.

When God speaks something into your spirit, it is like something has just been conceived. It could be a dream, vision, strategy even a business venture. When God speaks something into your heart you have a decision to make. What will you do with what God has placed in your heart? Will you let that dream die, because it seems implausible or even impossible to achieve, or will you fight for what God has deposited into your heart? Will you let doubt, fear, lack of resources and lack of experience destroy the tiny promises that is gestating in your heart? Or will you fight for and contend for the fullness of it to come forth in its perfect time and season? The choice is yours. In every situation you have opportunity to make a decision to contend.

John 10:10 reminds us that Satan's assignment is threefold; to kill, steal and destroy. He wants to steal and destroy your hopes, dreams, and all that God has promised you. This is much like the attack against the first born sons of Moses' time. In an attempt to kill Moses as an infant, Pharoh issued a death decree for all of the male babies to be murdered. Likewise, Satan knows that it is to his benefit to kill your dream at the level of infancy, before your dreams ever begins to grow, take shape and develop.

I like to call it an action plan, because the journey toward fulfilling your hopes and dreams will require, "faith in action."

The season for your hopes and dreams remaining hopes and dreams, and never reaching fulfillment is done! What good is dreaming big if none of your dreams ever become your reality? Dreams were not intended to remain dreams forever. You must move forward with turning those dreams into fulfilled plans and manifested destiny. You must take deliberate steps toward fulfilling your dreams. I like to call it an action plan, because the journey toward fulfilling your hopes and dreams will require, "faith in action."

Dreams were not intended to remain dreams forever. You must move forward with turning those dreams into fulfilled plans and manifested destiny.

The Strategy

A powerful way to contend is through prayer. A consistent prayer life is an exceptional foundation for any decision, dream or venture. Below is a description of types of prayer that position us to earnestly contend in faith.

1. The Prayer of Agreement. Pray and confess in agreement with Heaven. Explore the following question. What does God say about the matter? Your confessions should always line up with what God's Word says and not with fear, doubt, worry

Standing on the Promises

or the appearance of our circumstance. Through the prayer of agreement you come into a place of agreement with God and with others. Your prayer power is multiplied because of the power that agreement with God releases. You are called to see through the eyes of faith and your confession and prayers should align with that. What you decree shall be established (Job 22:28). Do not be afraid to open up your mouth and speak. Your words are powerful, decree positively and in agreement with heaven. Call those things that have not yet manifested into existence.

2. Pray in Faith and Believe. Do you have the faith to believe God for what He has spoken, even if it seems impossible? A God-given vision should be one that requires God's intervention to bring to fulfillment. Do not think for a moment that you must accomplish and figure out everything on your own. You are not called to reach your dreams alone, do it with God's help and infinite wisdom. When you pray, pray in faith and believe that God will answer you and release the answer or strategy that you need. "Call upon Me and I will answer you and show you great and mighty things that you know not," (Jeremiah 33:3). Call upon God in faith! You should never be surprised when God answers you, that should be your expectation. Need an intervention? A divine intervention is the best intervention there is. Open up your mouth and invite God into the situation. He is ready and willing to partner with you to bring about His will in your life.

3. Pray the Word. What does the God's Word say about your situation? Isaiah 55:10-11 tells us that "God's Word shall not return void, but shall accomplish all that He sent it to do." It shall accomplish. When God releases a word, that word has an assignment of fulfillment attached to it. A promise from God is sure and shall come to past in its perfect time and season. God's Word cannot fail. It is the best place to take your stand. What better roadmap to guide your every step! The bible should

be the manual and guide for your life. It behooves you to be intimately familiar with the truths therein. The Word of God is referenced as a double edged sword. That is your sharpest weapon in contending with every adversary. Wield the sword of the Lord, which is the Word of God. Your footing is a major key in a wrestling match. Stand firm on the Word of God and meditate on the promises therein. It will help prevent you from being tossed to and fro by the storms and winds of life.

4. Persevere in Prayer. Do not be deterred or dismayed if the answer you are seeking does not come overnight or even after some days, weeks, months or years. Be committed to persevere in prayer and faith. Remember Jacob in Genesis 32 wrestled all night, because he was determined to receive the blessing. Abraham and Sarah waited many years before obtaining their promise of a son. Anna waited over sixty years for her promise to arrive. Though you may not physically pray all night long, your heart should be in a place where it is steadfast and does not move from that place of faith and trust in God. Persevere and refuse to give up on what God has spoken concerning your life! Continue to believe and stand in faith, even if the fulfillment of your promise is delayed.

5. Focused Prayer. Focus on God and the promise, not the circumstance and the problem. Look to God for the solution. He is a way-maker, a problem-solver and so much more. Even when it seems like there is no solution or way out, God is able to create something out of seeming nothingness and bring forth your solution. Focus on the problem-solver rather than the problem. No matter how great the problem may seem, God is greater.

Hannah Contended

Hannah, found in 1 Samuel Chapters 1-2, was a woman of great faith. I first found her life story inspiring while my husband and I battled with infertility prior to the birth of our first child. Hannah was a woman who refused to be denied. She held tightly to her promise, even in the face of stiff opposition.

Let's take a look at Hannah's journey to receiving the promises of God for her life and family. There was a man named Elkanah, who lived in the hill country of Ephraim. Elkanah had two wives, one named Penniah and one named Hannah. Every year during the time of feasts Elkanah traveled to the temple at Shiloh. There he worshipped the Lord and offered sacrifices. Every year Penniah and Hannah went with him. Now, Penniah had children, but Hannah had none for the Lord had closed her womb (1 Samuel 1:5). Hannah dealt with the shame and pain of not being able to give her husband a son, or any children at all. Hannah desperately desired to have children and she carried the burden of barrenness everywhere that she went. Penniah, her husband's other wife, was fertile and fruitful. She gave Elkanah children and to make matters worse Penniah taunted, persecuted and ridiculed Hannah because of her inability to have children. Penniah treated Hannah with disdain her actions were cruel and insensitive to say the least.

Hannah desperately desired to have children and she carried the burden of barrenness everywhere that she went.

Year after year they went up to the temple to worship, and year after year it was the same scenario. Penniah taunted and persecuted Hannah as they went. Penniah represented Hannah's adversary. What an adversary she was! Not only was Hannah battling discouragement and disappointment from her own barrenness, but she also had to deal with her husband's other wife persecuting her ruthlessly. Hannah's adversary sought to stand in her way and keep her from ever reaching the place of fulfilled promises. Hannah's adversary wanted to keep her in a prison of discouragement, depression and hopelessness. Hannah could have quit, given up and gone back home. All would have understood. Her womb was barren, her life full of heartache and pain, but something within her would not let her quit. There was a deep determination and hope in God that spurred her onward.

Every time Hannah looked at Penniah she was reminded of her own barren state and unfulfilled promise. It is so hard to see someone receive their promise when yours is still far from being fulfilled. This was Hannah's reality as she watched her husband's other wife bearing his children. The Lord had closed Hannah's womb. Hannah was not experiencing this season of barrenness because of something she had done wrong. This was part of the plan and timing of God for Hannah's life, because of her willingness to press and contend that barrenness was destined to be broken off her life. Hannah did not realize it, but she was contending and fighting to bring forth greatness. Eventually Hannah conceived and brought forth Samuel, a prophet and judge who would one day anoint kings. At times you may wonder why it seems so hard to conceive and bring forth the vision that you know God placed in your heart. It could be that like Hannah you are called to birth and establish greatness in the earth. Therefore, you must press past opposition and seasons of delay, with a bold commitment to what God has placed in your heart and spoken concerning your life. You must cling to the promises of God. Refuse to quit. Refuse to be denied for the promises of God are sure and shall not return void (Isaiah 55:11). It does not matter if you experience seasons of difficulty, lack, barrenness, hopelessness and discouragement. If God spoke something into your heart, you can bank on it! God is not a man that He should lie, neither the son of man that he should change His mind (Numbers 23:19 KJV).

> ***It is so hard to see someone receive their promise when yours is still far from being fulfilled.***

Standing on the Promises

It would have been so easy for Hannah to turn around and go back home. Penniah provoked Hannah until she wept bitterly and refused to eat. However, in 1 Samuel 1:9 we see a powerful shift.

Hannah Stood Up

"This went on year after year. Whenever Hannah went up to the house of the Lord, her rival provoked her till she wept and would not eat. Her husband Elkanah would say to her, "Hannah, why are you weeping? Why don't you eat? Why are you downhearted? Don't I mean more to you than ten sons?" Once when they had finished eating and drinking in Shiloh, Hannah stood up. Now Eli the priest was sitting on his chair by the doorpost of the Lord's house," (1 Samuel 1:7-9 NIV).

The above passage says that Hannah stood up. That is critically important. Penniah taunted and provoked Hannah severely, so badly that bitter tears streamed down Hannah's face and heart-sickness swept over her, which prevented her from even eating at the feast. After this cruel phase of persecution, the Bible says that Hannah stood up.

Have you ever seen two people getting ready to fight? I imagine that is how the scene looked. Hannah reached the place where she refused to be mistreated any longer. I imagine she reached the place where she said, "Enough is enough. I have had just about all I am going to take from you," and she stood up. What a scene! Yay, to all of the Hannah's in the world! Many of us need to get to the place where we say enough is enough and we take a stand against our adversaries!

When Hannah stood up, suddenly the tables turned. Now, Hannah towered over her adversary instead of cowering in shame or being bullied into that place of hopelessness and despair. When Hannah stood up, Penniah must have realized that something shifted, because the Bible does not say that Penniah uttered another wayward word after Hannah stood up. When Hannah stood up, she stood up on the promises of God for her life! Beloved if this story speaks to your heart I encourage you to take a stand like Hannah. Refuse to sit down in the midst of what your situation looks like, stop wallowing in the pit of who has done you wrong, stand up and plant your feet firmly on the infallible truth of God's Word.

Determined and Desperate

Hannah finally got to the place where she was delivered from people. She was determined, desperate and delivered from people. What a powerful combination when channeled in the proper way! Hannah asserted her efforts toward achieving her promise. The hurtful words, which could have discouraged her actually propelled her forward. She developed a resolve to not quit and to obtain God's promises no matter what. Hannah laid it all on the line. She didn't care who was looking. She didn't care what others thought. She didn't care anymore about the shame of barrenness that followed her everywhere. With great desperation Hannah prayed the very prayer that changed her entire existence. At that moment, Hannah had no idea that she was just moments away from breaking out of the realm of barrenness, and into the place of manifested destiny and fulfilled promises.

> ***Hannah finally got to the place where she was delivered from people. She was determined, desperate and delivered from people. What a powerful combination when channeled in the proper way!***

Jehovah Sabbaoth

Hannah prayed to the Lord Almighty also known as Jehovah Sabbaoth. She knew who God was and she called on Jehovah Sabbaoth, the Lord of heaven's armies, the one who will fight your battles. She called out and asked Him to come to her rescue. Hannah could have called on Jehovah Raphe the

Lord her healer, or Jehovah Shalom the Lord her peace, or even Jehovah Jireh the Lord her provider, but instead Hannah stood up and called on Jehovah Sabbaoth. Jehovah Sabbaoth, the Lord of heaven's armies is a name of God that describes His infinite resources and His warring, all-sufficient, beyond measure nature. Hannah called on the greatest contender of all! Hannah knew only God could help her and when she called, He answered. She prayed to God earnestly. He fought her battle and the decree of barrenness was broken off her life!

Chapter 12: Reality Strikes

A few years after my dream about leaping off the mountain (shared in this book Introduction,) I came face to face with the reality of that dream. That dream seemed to haunt me for years as I wondered what mountain I would be required to ascend and depart. The thought of leaping off a mountain into a totally new place frightened me terribly, and I pushed the very thought into a distant corner of my mind. In 2010 I gave birth to Gabrielle, our second daughter. That in itself was a miraculous experience that I will share more about in chapter twenty-one. After Gabrielle's birth, I began to hear the Lord speak to me concerning going in a new direction. For ten years, I worked as a psychiatric nurse in a child and adolescent mental health facility, and I wondered if the time was coming for a new start.

For over a year, I heard the Lord speak to my heart about leaving work. I chalked this up as a great impossibility. I ignored the preposterous thought, wrestled with it even rationalized all of the reasons why I could not possibly resign from work. In the middle of a recession when many Americans were suffering financially, seeking employment and better employment. Many people were desperate for good jobs, willing to stand for hours on end at career fairs, interviews and at the doorsteps of offices seeking employment. How could I walk away from a perfectly great job with great pay and wonderful benefits? My husband and I had a four year old and a new baby. It just seemed absurd to even think about leaving work. However, the unction persisted. I tried harder to ignore it. We even added up the numbers to see if we could afford financially for me to come out of work, we could not afford it. I could not see any possible way that we could take this step and stay afloat.

I prayed that God would make His plans perfectly clear to me, and that He would give my husband and I the strength to do all that He was requiring of us. I even told God that if He really, really, really wanted me to leave work, I trusted Him and would do it. That was one of the most difficult prayers I ever prayed. In the back of my mind I was praying that my situation would be like Abraham's in that my surrender and my yes would be enough. I was hoping that I would not have to go all the way through with sacrificing my job. You must understand. My husband was self-employed and our trucking business was already feeling the painful effects of the worsening economic recession. The very thought of my family suffering lack, because I left work was agonizing to even consider and that was something I never wanted to experience. Agonized is the perfect word to describe the inner battle I felt. As a Christian I knew I should have faith, but I agonized over this decision and shed many tears. I did not want my family to suffer a single day, on account of my decision. I hoped that the unction to go in a new direction would pass, but it didn't. It only grew stronger.

My husband was supportive despite the many unknowns. On one occasion he asked, "So tell me again why you are considering leaving work?"

I know that his faith was challenged when I answered hesitantly "well, because God told me to."

I know that my husband was worried, though he did not show it. He took a stand of faith and he encouraged me despite the long list of unknowns. He did not try to talk me out of my decision, instead he supported me and encouraged me along the way. He worked so hard to make ends meet, and most of all He trusted God every step of the way. At times, my faith wavered and it seemed that fear was winning the war against me. However, every time Tony was right there, to ease my fears and encourage my heart.

A Fight to the Death

This decision had been a thorn in my side for months. I felt like Jacob as I wrestled with knowing that I needed to surrender to God yet carefully the natural factors. I wanted to make sure I heard God correctly. I did not want to make a foolish mistake, at the same time I knew that I had to do what God was requiring of me. So, I settled into a place that many of us are familiar with, I procrastinated. I waited and waited and waited. I really believe I was supposed to resign from employment in April when I gave birth to Gabby. Unfortunately, April 2010 turned into June, which turned into August, October and finally January 2011.

Goodbye Will

My final decision was not birthed out of a strong faith-filled "yes." In my spiritual immaturity I had not reached a place of fully taking God at His word. I did not take a flying leap out onto the infallible strength and truth of God's Word. I did not say, "Ok God I hear you calling so I humbly surrender." This was more like a fight to the death. That is just what happened, a vicious fight to the death ensued. I fought, wrestled and rationalized daily. A fight to the death, there were some things in me that needed to die before I could go forward in complete faith and trust to take such a leap of faith. I had some mindsets that needed to be renewed or changed. I was looking to my job as our source of income and support. That is what so many people do. It is easy to believe that our jobs and the economic conditions determine and govern our finances. Sure, those factors impact our provision, but those things are not the origin of our sustenance. It was erroneous of me to think that my job was the "source" of our provision. I had to have a mindset shift. Yes, the job was an avenue of income, but I learned quickly that ultimately God is our source.

See, a leap of faith requires faith but faith was something that I lacked. I was more focused on the circumstances around me and economic conditions, than the word God spoke to my heart. When you launch out and do something your efforts must be carried out in faith. For me, taking that great leap from the security of employment was, indeed a fight to the death. Fear caused me to hold on and procrastinate for many months. My fears, pride, doubt, selfishness and much more needed to just curl up and die so that I could give God a genuine "yes" and go forward. It would have been easy to leave my job if I was leaving it for another job, or a better job, but the truth was I didn't know why I was leaving work! Only that I was following God's leading. Once my will and all of my excuses had been laid to rest, I mustered a tiny bit of faith, I believe mustard seed faith is what they call it, and that was all I had. I reluctantly took the leap that loomed before me.

After my departure from employment, God revealed powerfully to my husband and me that He alone is our source, not our paychecks, employers or businesses. He alone is our source and it is He who will supply all of our needs according to his riches in glory (Philippians 4:19). Job or no job, God will provide. That was the bottom line that I had to believe and embrace.

My will had to die. Oh it's easy to say, but when it comes down to it are you willing to surrender your will completely to God. The apostle Paul said it best when he declared, "I die daily," (1 Corinthians 15:31). Is the Bible recommending a daily physical death? No, instead there must be a willingness to lay down your will, mindsets and fears to receive and embrace God's perfect will and direction for your life. Your flesh and mindsets must submit and come into agreement with God. Paul made it so clear when he said, "I die daily." This indicates the need to deal with your flesh on a consistent basis, a daily basis. To check your flesh occasionally is not enough. Paul admonished all to deal with your flesh and fleshly desires daily. Your flesh, fears and mindsets can surely hinder you from walking in obedience and faith.

Facing the Unknowns

A challenging area in this life journey is facing the unknowns. There are so many unknowns in life. I am sure life would be easier if you always knew where you were going and how God was working things out in your life. However, if you knew all the answers and could work out every situation for yourself there would be little reason to trust in God. Despite all of the unknowns, we must be committed to trusting God and walking by faith. As I walked away from my career, the unknowns were so frightening. I did not know how we would survive financially. I did not know fully why I was leaving or where I was going. If I had another job lined up, it would have provided the comfort and security I desired with this transition. Instead I had a list of unknowns longer than you could imagine.

Get to the place where you stop trying to figure it all out, and start trusting God.

In life you will face unknowns. As you go forward, do not allow the things that you do not know to cause you to walk in fear and bondage. God does not require you to know everything, but He does expect you, to trust and obey Him. If you are in the process of pursuing your purpose, hopes and dreams keep your eyes on God. Focus on what He has deposited in your heart. Allow Him to order your steps and open doors of opportunity and blessing for you. Get to the place where you stop trying to figure it all out, and start trusting God.

It was during this season of transition that a saying arose in my heart. It brought great strength and courage to me and I still stand on this truth. The saying is, *"God I don't know how you are going to do it, but I know and trust that you are going to do just what you said."*

It is not your job to figure out the "how's" and "when's." Your job is to trust God, stand on His promises and walk in His will. When you do this you can expect that He will perform His word in your life and bring you into a place of fulfilled hopes and dreams.

Despise Not the Stretching

There are times in life when God may test your faith to the limit, or what feels like your limit. There are times when the test of your faith may seem to far exceed your limit! However, you must realize that your perceived limit and God's limit are probably quite different. He knows how much you can bear. In times when you feel like you are being stretched beyond your capacity, and feel you will break or rip in two if something does not give, take comfort in knowing that His stretching is for your good! God stretches your faith to enlarge your faith! Without stretching we will never move beyond our zone of comfort and venture out into new territory. What is it that you have been turning over and over in your mind, considering venturing into? Have you hesitated, because your fear outweighs your faith?

God stretches your faith to enlarge your faith!

My Dad's a Superhero

Some think that faith must be enormous and mature, but in fact God looks for child-like faith. "Except ye come as little children ye shall in no ways enter the Kingdom of Heaven," (Matthew 18:3 KJV). Children have an uncanny ability to believe. Our daughters still believe daddy is part superhero. They believe that he can do absolutely anything. They believe their daddy has all the money in the world and can meet their every need, whim and request no matter how large and of course do it at a moment's notice. They believe he has super-human strength and can lift or move anything including the car, clearly evidenced when Olivia asked him to pick up the car so she could get her ball. Their faith is precious and some would think it naïve, but in fact their faith is precisely the faith God desires all of us to have.

Luke 1:37 tells us that "with God all things are possible." That sums it up perfectly. With God, all things are possible. Child-like faith can easily perceive and believe this truth. Have total confidence in God. He is all-knowing, all-powerful and loves you in such a way that is beyond comprehension. God has limitless supply and resource. All of this is available to you as the Lord wills, because you are one of His children. Just as a parent cares for every need and hunger of their child, God will care for and fulfill all of your needs according to His riches in glory!

Many people who experience struggles and tests of faith develop callousness in their hearts limiting their ability to believe. The willingness to believe becomes more difficult. Fear of further disappointment causes some to withdraw or put up imaginary walls. Some have been so bruised by disappointments that they find it too painful to keep on believing. Be reminded today that delay is not denial. Just because something does not come forth in the time you anticipated, if God promised it keep on believing. If you are one who has struggled with disappointment, please pray the following prayer with me. God wants to heal you of every hurt and wound. Let the healing process begin today.

Personal Prayer

Dear Lord, thank You for loving me so perfectly. I ask You now to heal my heart. Heal every hurt, memory and disappointment, even the hurts and disappointments from my childhood. Heal every memory and help me to believe again. Help me to believe that the promises of God are for my life. Help me to tear down every self-erected wall. I repent for walking in doubt and fear. Help me to trust you completely. Help me to live in faith, not fear. Right now I choose to release all hurt and disappointment from my past and I go forward in victory! In Jesus Name, Amen!

Chapter 13: Obedience

God may instruct you to do something that is beyond your zone of comfort. It may seem silly, absurd, or even heart wrenching and grievous. We find an interesting interaction between God and Abraham in Genesis chapter 22. God gave Abraham a directive that many people would struggle with. God told him to journey up to Mount Moriah and offer his beloved son, Isaac as a sacrifice. God tested Abraham's faith and obedience. Would Abraham trust God with what was most precious to him? God spoke great promises to Abraham, but on the road to fulfillment stood a tremendous test of faith and obedience. Abraham's responses of faith and obedience impacted generations powerfully through the release of generational blessings. "In you all the families of the earth shall be blessed," (Genesis 12:3).

Abraham was asked to sacrifice his only son. For many years, Abraham and Sarah prayed and believed God for Isaac. Their promise was finally safe in their arms, now Abraham was instructed to sacrifice him and give him back to God. Did Abraham know this was a test? We do not know for sure. We do know that he was obedient and willing to do all that the Lord commanded him. Thankfully, during the final moments, as Abraham raised his hand over Isaac to sacrifice him, an angel appeared and brought word that sacrificing Isaac was not required. A ram in the bush was supplied instead. Abraham passed this great test of obedience.

Obedience Can Save Lives

I believe the Lord gives tests of obedience quite frequently. Many people ignore such tests or render partial obedience while some yield wholeheartedly to God and fully obey His leading. It could be as simple as a sudden desire to call a friend you have not seen in months. That sudden urge to reach out to that person could be the Holy Spirit prompting you. You do not know what that person is dealing with, but your call could brighten their day or even save their life. In fact I experienced that not too long ago.

Before discovering God's help, rest and renewal I went through an intense season of fighting to stay afloat. During that time I was exhausted, seemingly drowning and dangerously near the end of my rope. One particularly dreary day depression was knocking down my door and I was too weak to keep the door bolted. I felt so hopeless and helpless. Loneliness crept in and settled on me like a cloak. My mind taunted me, *"Why are you even here? What good are you to anyone? What's the point? Why not just give up?"* Me! A well-trained psychiatric nurse! I could not believe I was entertaining such thoughts. I knew I needed to pull myself quickly from this dangerous pity-party pit of despair, but I could not.

I sat there in that place of hopeless despair. My tears flowed like rivers until there were no more tears to flow. I sat in silence, clinging to one Scripture that had risen in my heart.

It was one of David's prayers. "Why art thou cast down, O my soul? And why art thou disquieted within me? Hope in God: for I shall yet praise him, who is the health of my countenance, and my God," (Psalm 42:5 KJV). Hope in God, hope in God. I murmured the words over and over clinging for dear life to the truth of these precious words. Hope was precisely what I needed.

The phone rang. The shrill ring broke the dead silence and despite a slew of thoughts against it, I answered the phone. It was Taiwan Brown, my prayer partner. Eleven hundred miles away, yet she felt led to pick up the phone and call me right at the moment I was entertaining thoughts of giving up. Right at that moment when it seemed the world was caving in around me, right at that moment, she called. I know that was orchestrated by God. I know it. That in itself was enough to strengthen my weary heart and let me know that God had not forgotten about me, and that I would pass through this place of testing. God has a way of sending help and encouragement at precisely the right time.

We prayed together and the depression, discouragement and helplessness lifted once and for all. Oh what a blessing it is to have a prayer partner. If you do not have a prayer partner, I encourage you to ask God to show you that person. Who is it that will stand in agreement with you and pray, fast and believe God with you for His will and promises to be fulfilled in your life?

The Power of Prayer

So Taiwan called, right on time. She has a way of being right on time. We have been prayer partners since 2004. My dear friend and mentor, Shandi Starks, introduced us. I will be forever grateful to Shandi for all that she has invested in my life, and for encouraging Taiwan and I to connect. All of these years Taiwan has lived in Texas and I, in North Carolina, and yet we are the best of friends and most of all we support each other consistently in prayer. A prayer partner does not have to be someone that you see. With prayer partners the connection is a spiritual one. Taiwan and I have prayed each other through all manner of crisis, illnesses, infertility, childbirth, marital struggles, career shifts and the list truly goes on and on. On that dreadful day in September she prayed me through thoughts of suicide. See, prayer is powerful.

Yes, I am a psychiatric nurse by profession. Yes, I encountered numerous people dealing with depression and suicidal tendencies and most of them needed years of therapy and possibly medication too. I am a great supporter of therapy and counseling, and I am not speaking against it in any way, but there isn't a therapy on earth that can compare to the healing power of God! On that day when my world seemed to be falling apart, God came to my rescue in an instant and drew me from that pit of despair. I know that the prayers of the righteous avail much. I know it. Those prayers elevated me out of that dungeon I was in and I experienced the love and renewal of God. Since then, it has been full steam ahead, no looking back. No other bouts with depression or hopelessness, only a renewed passion to help others experience the restoration and healing power of God. Whatever ails you, God is able to bring healing.

I am a great supporter of therapy and counseling, and I am not speaking against it in any way, but there isn't a therapy on earth that can compare to the healing power of God!

Just Ask Jonah

Obedience is not always easy, in many cases it is just the opposite. Obedience should stretch you beyond your zone of comfort and familiarity. When God requires something of you, your response is often connected to the salvation, breakthrough and deliverance of others. The obedience of one person can affect multitudes. Simply consider Jonah.

God gave Jonah a strategic mission, but it was one that Jonah wrestled in his heart to accept. He was sent to Nineveh to urge its population to repent. How bizarre the assignment sounded to him. His own people were sinking into a pit of despair that seemed to have no bottom, yet he was sent to save others. I believe Jonah dreaded the success of this mission far more than he dreaded failure. His own people needed divine intervention just as much as Nineveh. So, Jonah attempted to run from this call.

What was Jonah's response to God's call? He ran. Jonah attempted to run and hide from God, taking refuge in the belly of a boat. He was later swallowed up by a great fish and found himself in the belly of that fish with nowhere else to run. Jonah was forced to face himself and God. Many can relate to Jonah. There are times when God gives an assignment that may not agree with your flesh. It may be contrary to what you desire to do. Yet, that does not excuse you from the assignment. Successful obedience leads to open doors and greater opportunities. Every assignment will not be comfortable, but your obedience is still required. A great key of successful advancement is obeying God.

Trust and Obey

When God tells you to go or gives you an assignment that seems beyond your capacity, rejoice. God has already made provision for you and will see you through the process. God does not call you and then abandon you. Moses recognized this and told God that he would only go if God went with him (Exodus 33:15). This should be your posture as well. Have you ever launched out on your own, and then looked for God's safety net, as you began to stumble and flounder? You must seek Him before ever taking the first step and then go forward as He leads you. "The steps of a good man are ordered by the Lord," (Psalm 37:23). This means that your path has already been set, planned and ordered. The text does not say that God will order your steps. It says that God has ordered your steps. It is already done. When you walk in obedience to God you walk in a path that has been ordered for your life. Often times the path of success and blessing is the road less traveled. In fact, if you are a Christian who is committed to serving God with your life you can expect that your path will be the road less traveled.

"Enter through the narrow gate. For wide is the gate and broad is the road that leads to destruction, and many enter through it. But small is the gate and narrow the road that leads to life, and only a few find it," (Matthew 7:13-14 NIV). As a believer, your path is not usually the popular path or the comfortable path. Yet, it is the path of righteousness, holiness and obedience.

Your life should be a testament of God's goodness, grace and saving power. When others see you they should desire to know why you do not fit in with the rest of the crowd. God did not put you on this earth to fit in with the crowd. Your obedience to God is greater than being liked or fitting in with the majority. Be willing to take a stand for what is right.

Overcoming the Fear of Failure

The fisherman in Luke chapter 5 were wearied and discouraged, after a long night of fishing their nets were empty and they seriously considered quitting. They had labored all night long and caught no fish. They were battling despair until Jesus walked into their situation and released the word that brought forth their miracle. Jesus stepped right into their boat and began to teach from that boat. Before He told the fisherman to launch out and try again, He spoke into their situation. We too must look for the word of God in the midst of our situations. In the midst of every situation, ask God for direction. What is His will for you? God's instruction is always the best instruction, although it may challenge your faith.

God's instruction is always the best instruction, although it may challenge your faith.

When Jesus was done teaching from the boat He told them to go out where the water was deeper and let down their nets again. This required faith and corresponding action from the fisherman. They had already fished all night long with no success, they had already come up empty-handed, they were wearied and discouraged and then Jesus instructed them to launch out into the deep and try it all over again. The fishermen had a decision to make. Would they trust Jesus or allow the word to pass them by? The fisherman rallied their faith and obeyed.

Simon answered Jesus saying, "We have toiled all night and caught nothing, nevertheless at your word I will let down the net," (Luke 5:5 NKJV).

Oh, I believe that is a word for many. Many need to declare, "Nevertheless at your word dear Lord, I will obey." It may seem like things have not gone your way but "nevertheless at your word Lord." It may seem like you have been struggling for a long time with no progress but "nevertheless at your word." You must take God at His word and trust Him to perform His word in your life!

Be diligent about recognizing the adversary's tactics. John 10:10 tells us Satan comes to kill, steal and destroy. Satan does not want to see you succeed and will use tactics such as discouragement, fear, weariness, sabotage and doubt to cause you to miss what God desires to do and release in your life. You must also have an ear to hear what the Spirit of God is saying to you.

God is releasing strategy, but you must be deliberate in your efforts to listen and spend time in prayer and fasting to hear what the Lord is saying.

Fear of failure is a force that wars against believers and nonbelievers alike. It is the fear of failure that hinders many people from ever starting something new, such as a new job or opportunity. They do not even launch out to see if they will succeed or fail, because that fear paralyzes and casts such a negative light, that it hinders them from accepting the offer or taking the first step. Fear has opposed the righteous for too long and I encourage you to take authority over it in your own life. Serve fear an eviction notice and go forward into your purpose! 1 John 4:18 tells us that perfect love evicts fear. Where the perfect love of God abounds, fear cannot remain. Pray for all fear to be flooded out of your life, by the perfect love of God. Then go forward victoriously in all that He has called you to do.

> ***Fear has opposed the righteous for too long and I encourage you to take authority over it in your own life.***

Try Again

There must be a willingness to try again when success is not achieved initially. Many people become terribly discouraged and hurt when things do not go the way they initially hoped and far too many give up prematurely. God clearly shows us in Luke chapter 5 that you must be willing to trust God and try again. Could God have allowed the fishermen to bring in a miraculous catch of fish the very first time they cast their nets? Absolutely, but He orchestrated this in such a way that their faith and obedience were tested. Many people could have done like the fishermen and cast those nets the first time. However, could you have cast those nets again after a long season of complete failure? That was the plight of the fishermen. They fished all night to no avail. Jesus challenged them at the point of their faith and instructed them to try again. Is that a word for you as well? Is the Lord encouraging you to try again? Do not allow the fear of failure to stop you. Be willing to let down your nets again. Be willing to try again even if you do not achieve your desired results at first. Trust God completely and "cast your net" with faith and expectancy.

God was preparing the fishermen to be fishers of men and failure had to be dealt with and overcome from the very onset. Jesus had to prepare them for the discouragement they would face, and make sure they were willing to persevere and not give up, as they went forth preaching the Gospel and saving souls. Jesus knew lives would be at stake not just fish, and these men had to be willing to "cast their nets again" again and again, sending out the Gospel and bringing in the souls.

Without faith it is impossible to please God (Hebrews 11:6). You must not go through life void of faith. When you have faith there must be action to accompany it. You are called to move from faith to faith and glory to glory. Your capacity to believe God should progressively increase, not dwindle. Remember, "faith comes by hearing and hearing by the word of God," (Romans 10:17). Therefore, you must position yourself to hear and partake of God's Word regularly. Read your Bible regularly. It is the roadmap for your life.

Chapter 14: Learning to Rest in Him

I stood on the edge of a cliff. Don't ask me how I got there. I just did. The icy wind whipped thru my hair and stung my face. Tears pressed their way from my eyes. I looked up ahead. The ground had run out. My feet rested at the edge of the cliff. The clouds were my equals, facing me eye to eye and surrounding me completely. I felt sure that if I lifted my hand it would disappear in the billowy mist. I looked over the cliff's edge and my heart rose in my chest. The earth below was barely visible. How did I get to this place, teetering on the edge of this jagged cliff, thousands of feet in the air? Tears stung my eyes and I quickly wiped them away with the back of my hand. I took several deep breaths attempting to gather my bearings.

All was eerily silent except for the wind. The wind howled and whistled around me, the clouds watched. My feet, covered in worn sneakers, took a tentative step closer to the edge of the cliff. The frigid wind picked up and caused my blue jacket to flap in the breeze. I stood on the edge of the cliff. The clouds watched, likely wondering about my next move. Thoughts raced through my head as I pondered what I should do. Go forward or turn around and go back the way I came? I closed my eyes and did the unthinkable. I took a step forward off the edge of the cliff.

I fell. It seemed like an eternity. My hands grasped frantically around me in the cloudy mist. I fell hard, but something stopped my fall. I landed on a flat surface. *What had stopped my fall? Why hadn't I fallen to the waiting earth below?* I rested on my knees, my chest heaved and I struggled to catch my breath. I looked up ahead and saw the clouds had thinned and parted enough for me to see my surroundings. A bridge had appeared seemingly out of thin air. Instead of falling thousands of feet to the earth below, a bridge appeared and I landed securely on it. To my amazement the bridge was rather sturdy. Still shaken, I looked up to the heavens and a hesitant smile crossed my lips. Surely God must be with me. Surely He must.

Suddenly I heard a voice calling my name. I looked to the heavens again as I heard my name called so clearly.

I heard it again. "Christina, it's time." I rose to my feet, standing on the bridge in the sky. Then I heard it again, "Christina, it's time." I heard it a third time, but this time I felt the gentle shake of my husband's hand. "Christina, it's time to wake up," he said warmly.

It had all been a dream, but one that would remain engrained in my heart. This was another dream with deep and significant meaning.

Later that morning, I spent time listening for the Lord to speak some insight and understanding about that dream. I remembered well the feel of the wind whipping around me and, the clouds that seemed so near, the height of the cliff and the feeling of hopelessness as I looked at the vast nothingness before me. In the dream I was following a certain path, but the ground had run out. It seemed there was nowhere to go. Go back the way I had come? Or take a step forward, even though the road had run out? Which way was I to go? I was intrigued by this dream as I sought the Lord for understanding. I desperately wanted to know its meaning.

A Message in the Night

The Lord clearly spoke the following words to my heart regarding this dream: *There are times when you feel like you have come to the end of your road. You have done everything you know how to do, and still cannot see how you can go forward. There are times when it seems you are facing a sea of impossibility. The thought of retreating or even hiding in a cave weighs heavily on you, though you know that is not the prescribed path for your life. Know that you are not alone and when you face a sea of impossibility and stand obediently in faith, I will create a bridge for you in the midst of impossibility. Where it seems there is no way, I will release a new way.*

I buried my face in my hands as these words washed over me. The tears came. The God of heaven was keenly aware of my situation and had spoken so plainly to my deepest worries.

It goes without saying that you would likely struggle to trust someone you do not know, and therein lies the secret of learning to trust God. In life you may find yourself struggling to trust other people because of their flaws, failures and inconsistencies. Even people who you love, admire or are bonded with in covenant relationships may receive only marginal trust from you because of past hurts, violations and abuses of trust. Thankfully, you do not have to worry about any such abuses of your trust with God. The willingness to trusting God is birthed out of knowing Him. In order to securely rest in a place of confidently trusting God, you must know Him in a personal way. Trusting God follows naturally, when you understand who He is.

Worthy of Your Trust

You should trust God, because He is God and He is worthy of your trust. Unlike the tendencies of men, God never lies and never fails to fulfill His promises.

> "God is not a man, that he should lie; neither the son of man, that he should repent: hath he said, and shall he not do it? or hath he spoken, and shall he not make it good?" (Numbers 23:19 KJV). Unlike men, God has the power to accomplish all that He has promised and spoken. He always makes good on His promises. The Lord Almighty has sworn, 'Surely, as I have planned so it will be, and as I have purposed so it will happen," (Isaiah 14:24 NIV). Furthermore, God's plans are perfect, holy, and righteous and He works all things together for good for those who love Him and are called according to His holy purpose (Romans 8:28).

The choice to trust in God should be obvious, but far too often people struggle to trust God completely, because they do not know Him. They know of God, but have not opened their hearts to receive Him. They have not formed a personal relationship with Him. The very first step in developing this relationship is to invite Him in to your heart. Open your heart to the Lord. Further develop this relationship with the Lord through prayer, studying His Word and spending time in His presence. As you commune with the Lord and deepen your relationship with Him, trust will become much easier. It is so much easier to trust someone who you know and love, and when you know that have your best interests as heart

Knowing God

Getting to know God can be approached quite simply. When you want to get to know someone, you spend time with them and communicate with them. The same is true with God. Talk to God, just as you would talk to a dear friend.

My daughter, Olivia, asked me an interesting question this morning.

She looked at me and asked, "Mom, what's God's phone number?"

I tried to hide my amusement and I responded quite seriously, "Why do you ask?"

She answered with complete faith, "Because I want to call Him. I have a question to ask Him."

Oh, that should encourage your faith! Olivia believed that if she picked up the phone and dialed the right number, God would answer and engage in a conversation with her. She completely expected to be able to reach God and she completely expected that He would respond! We can call on God anytime, but many of us fail to do so. With great joy I shared with Olivia that she is able to talk to God any time she desires. We had a wonderful conversation about prayer and communicating with God. Child-like faith is absolutely precious.

How do we get to know God? Communicate with Him through prayer and listening to His voice. Spend glorious time with Him through worship, reading and meditating on His Word. Carve out time for God in your busy schedule and guard that God-time fiercely. Spend time with God. That should be a priority in your life, not an afterthought. God has not made Himself difficult to find or know. If you seek Him, you will find Him. Indeed learning to trust is a process, but as you spend time with the Lord and get to know Him, your trust in Him will blossom. Trust is at the heart of the matter. Will you trust God even when life does not work out the way you hoped? I am convinced that most of life's frustrations are really lessons in trusting God.

Faith Opens the Door

A few years ago while in a church worship service the Spirit of God moved powerfully and a great outpouring of His magnificent glory was released in our midst. People praised and rejoiced and as the glory came in many were falling prostrate on the floor, unable to stand in the weighty presence of God's glory. During the service an invitation was given for any unsaved persons to receive salvation. I fully expected the altar to be flooded with people.

The word had been powerful and one that causes the hearts of man to reflect upon their lives and seek opportunity to get things right with God. However, during the invitation for salvation two small girls walked down to the altar. That was all two small girls maybe seven or eight years old. I rejoiced and was exceedingly glad for those two souls, but I wondered where the rest were? I heard the Lord speak to my heart about those two girls that they were a prophetic sign for the church. I felt a sudden urge to find out their names. I did not hesitate.

Immediately following the service, I sought out the young girls. I found the counselor who was ministering to them and I asked their names. The counselor shared that only one girl came forward for salvation. The other was already saved and came with her for support. The girl who came forward for salvation was named Destiny. The girl who accompanied her was named Imani (which can mean Faith). The prophetic sign was clear. On that day Faith opened the door for Destiny, and Faith ushered Destiny into the house.

Likewise, your faith opens the door of your destiny and it is by faith that you are able to discover, apprehend and enter into the destiny created for your life. Each and every person has a God-ordained destiny, and that pathway is laden with promises. In fact, your destiny is one of the great promises God has for your life. It is up to you to walk out that path with faith and obedience. When your way seems uncertain, you must look to God for direction and clarity. He holds the answers and He holds the master keys to every door you must past through. He holds the answers to every test you will take in life. Go wants to show you the way to your purpose and lead you on a victorious path of fulfillment. You don't have to know everything about where you are headed. Learn to rest in Him and follow His leading. Don't expect Him to reveal all the details. That is why your faith is required. Rest in Him.

Likewise, your faith opens the door of your destiny and it is by faith that you are able to discover, apprehend and enter into the destiny created for your life.

How sweet it is to know that no matter what you are going thru, no matter what you are facing, God is keenly aware of your situation. He knows your end from the beginning. He knows your outcome in every situation, and He has plans and purposes for you that will be revealed as you progress through life. Even in your darkest hour, God knows the plans that He has for you and they are plans for your good, to bring you to an expected end (Jeremiah 29:11). Even when you cannot see your outcome or destination, God can see it and He is ever mindful of it.

Let Your Hope Arise

In Jeremiah chapter 29 we find the Israelites in a hard place. After years of idolatrous worship and disobedience, Jeremiah was sent to them and used by God to prophesy judgment and the need for repentance. In chapter 29 the Israelites had been exiled and were facing despair. It was at that moment that God sent Jeremiah with the word of hope found in Jeremiah 29:11. In the

Standing on the Promises

midst of their suffering and isolation God sent a word of comfort to remind them of His great plans for their lives.

The Israelites were in danger of succumbing to hopelessness and despair because of their circumstance. Jeremiah called them to hear the word of the Lord.

Jeremiah 29:11 says, "For I know the plans I have for you," declares the Lord, "plans to prosper you and not to harm you, plans to give you hope and a future." Through this verse hope and strength were imparted to a people who had grown weary. God had not forgotten them nor forsaken them. He knew the course of their journey and He knew their expected end.

Likewise beloved, God has a plan and purpose for you. There is a set plan for your life and you are right in the midst of it. Even when you do not know the thoughts or plans God has for you, He does. Even when you cannot see your expected end, He can. He is in the midst of you and is ever working toward bringing you to your expected end.

Just Be

For thousands of years, God has called His servants to fulfill and carry out various missions and assignments. It is a misconception to think that one has to be a pastor or elder or other clergy to be called and used by God. God has endowed all mankind with specific assignments to fulfill. These assignments may span various arenas and sectors of society. There may be a governmental call upon your life. There is a great need for people of faith who will transform the political arena while upholding truth and righteousness without compromise. You may be called to do a groundbreaking work in the area of medicine. You may be called to care for, teach, and make a difference in the lives of children or on the mission fields of this nation or foreign lands. You may be called to serve as a great leader or visionary in the area of business and the marketplace. Whatever the specifics of your call, you do have a call. God has called you to make a difference in this world especially outside of the four walls of the church. Ministry was not intended to remain within the walls of the church. There is a call upon all believers to reach the lost. If you confine yourself to pews and four walls each Sunday, only allowing your light to shine in the boundaries of church settings, the lost will never get to experience the glorious power of Christ's love and salvation through you.

Do what God has placed in your heart to do, and be who He has called you to be. You are 100% original. Be that original person without apology. Allow the creative power of God to shine through you. God created you for greatness. Do not be ashamed or afraid to walk that path of greatness.

You are 100% original. Be that original person without apology.

Whatever it is that God has called you to, be diligent in carrying out the fullness of it. Never underestimate the value or significance of your assignment. If God has called you to it, then it is filled with purpose. It is God's will for you to carry out your ministry to the fullness.

Chapter 15: Honor Releases Breakthrough

Let's look at what the Bible says about honor and how this is directly connected to breaking through into a new place.

"Honor the Lord with thy substance and with the first fruits of all thine increase, so shall thy barns be filled with plenty and thy presses shall burst out with new wine," (Proverbs 3:9-10 KJV). This text paints a picture of what happens when you honor the Lord. This is a powerful passage that is filled with promise and instruction.

Honor the Lord with all that the Lord has given you and entrusted to your stewardship. Honor Him by giving back to Him with tithes, offerings and the first fruits of all your increase. Give of the good that is stored up in your life. Give to God from the treasury He has given to you. Do not limit your giving to monetary giving. You also honor the Lord by giving of your time, talents, resources and more.

Overtaxing Lack

When you honor the Lord you can expect to receive certain blessings as stated in Proverbs 3:9-10. When you honor the Lord you can expect to abide in a place of increase, a place that is running over with blessings. In life you may have experienced a time of favor or a situation where you received a blessing that was short-lived, but Proverbs 3:9-10 speaks of a different level of blessedness. Honor releases the flow of blessing and abundance where lack is overtaken by the favor of God. Your barns will be filled with plenty and you can expect to remain in that place of blessing. Once you open up the door for this level of blessing to flow in your life, you can expect that every dry place will be transformed, as rivers of blessing are released to flow in your life. Honor is a great key to dwelling in a place of victory and abundance.

Proverbs 3:9-10 says, "Your presses shall burst out with new wine." Bursting out denotes breaking through with force. It suggests that the blessings are coming with such force that they will break through barriers and flow out in abundance. To burst out speaks of breaking through into another place. Do you desire to break out of the place you are in and into a new place in God?

When you honor the Lord you can expect to experience breakthrough in your life in fact, honor will usher you into a place of breakthrough. Your barns or your accounts, storehouses, livelihood, and businesses shall be filled with plenty. Your presses or the labor of your hands shall burst out with new wine. In other words, great breakthrough and abundance will be released in your life with force. This is promised when you will honor the Lord with your substance and the first fruits of your increase.

Building a Lifestyle of Honor

There are other ways you can honor God. You can honor God through obedience and keeping His commandments. Treat others with love and respect. Build up people instead of tearing them down. Find the good in others instead of finding fault. When you honor others God is also honored.

If you want to see the promises of God manifest in your life, then honor God and honor His word. Let's talk about prophetic words. At times someone may speak a prophecy into your life and you discount it or do not receive it simply because of who delivered the message to you. You must learn to discern God in every situation. God can use whomever and whatever He chooses to get His message to you. If He can open up the mouth of a donkey, to tell Balaam about himself, then you better believe He can use anyone He chooses. So, even if you do not like the person you must discern if the message truly is from God. If it is truly a word from the Lord, and you do not believe it or cast it to the side, then you are dishonoring God.

You must learn to discern God in every situation.

Forever Changed

The most life changing prophetic word I have received to date came from a woman who was in a drug rehabilitation house. She was a middle-aged woman who had been ravaged by the trials of life. Her exterior was worn far past her years, but her spirit was beautiful and she had a keen ear to hear what the Lord was saying. One day the Holy Spirit came upon her powerfully during a church service. This was at a time in my life when I was totally asleep to my purpose and calling. I had no idea what God had called me to do in the earth. I had no idea that I would one day become a teacher, preacher, conference speaker and writer. This woman was consumed by the Holy Spirit and she spoke three words to me. No more and no less, three simple yet life-changing words. I will never forget that moment. By the time she finished her three word sentence I had fallen down under the power of God for most of the remainder of the service. After receiving those three words and having some glorious time while out on the carpet, I got up. The change in me was immediate. Something had shifted! My eyes had been opened. Suddenly, my feet had been transplanted onto the course of my destiny! Those three words catapulted me into my calling within a matter of days. That very night I began to dream of my purpose and destiny.

> ***Her exterior was worn far past her years, but her spirit was beautiful and she had a keen ear to hear what the Lord was saying.***

However, if I did not receive that word because of who she was or what she was going through I could have missed a pivotal moment. Remember, she was in a drug rehabilitation program at the time. Her appearance was unsightly and her reputation tarnished. Yet, she had a word from the Lord that radically shook me from my sleep and awakened me to my purpose. Had I discounted the word, because it did not come from a pastor or prophet, I could have missed out on a divine moment of opportunity and awakening.

When the prophetic word comes it can be likened to God writing you a letter or leaving you a voice mail. Think about that. Imagine if you just threw a letter from God away without even reading it or deleted the voicemail. When you fail to believe and receive God's word, even the prophetic word, you are dishonoring God. You must not be so concerned with the messenger that you miss the message that God is trying to convey to you.

He Speaks

What has God spoken concerning your life? What promises has He extended to you? God may reveal a promise to you, but if it does not come to past by the next week, do not allow doubt to creep in and steal your faith. Have you been speaking against your own dreams, because you lack the faith to believe them? If God said it, then you must stand on it and believe it. You must contend for that promise to come forth. A promise is a promise. God is not a man that He should lie, and His promises are yes and amen!

Have you been speaking against your own dreams, because you lack the faith to believe them?

"The earth was void, without form and darkness was everywhere. The Spirit of God was hovering over the face of the deep," (Genesis 1:2 NIV).

The earth was void and without form and something amazing happened, God spoke. There was nothing there. Darkness was everywhere and the earth had not yet been formed, and God spoke. The Holy Spirit hovered over the situation and God spoke. When God spoke the world was formed. He spoke the world into existence. How incredible! If God can speak the world into existence, surely He can speak life and victory into your situation.

Standing on the Promises

"So shall My word be that goes forth out of my mouth: it shall not return to Me void, but it shall accomplish that which I please and it shall prosper in the thing where I sent it," (Isaiah 55:11 KJV).

When God speaks and a word leaves His mouth there is an assignment attached to that word. God does not speak idle words or empty promises. When God speaks a promise or word to you it has an assignment of fulfillment attached to it. You must hold fast to the promises of God even in the face of opposition. The devil would love to see you give up and forfeit all that God has promised you. Just because your promise has not manifested yet does not mean it is not coming, remember the familiar saying that *delay is not denial*! Honor God with your faith. Hold fast to His word. You honor the promises of God when you believe, receive, and then contend for them to come to past.

When God speaks a promise or word to you it has an assignment of fulfillment attached to it.

Dishonor Halts the Flow of Blessing

"And when he was come into his own country, he taught them in their synagogue, insomuch that they were astonished, and said, Whence hath this man this wisdom, and these mighty works? Is not this the carpenter's son? Is not his mother called Mary? And his brethren, James, and Joseph, and Simon, and Judas? And his sisters, are they not all with us? Whence then hath this man all these things? And they were offended in him. But Jesus said unto them, A prophet is not without honor, save in his own country, and in his own house. And he did not many mighty works there because of their unbelief," (Matthew 13:54-58).

What an interesting situation. Jesus was confronted by familiarity in his own country. Those who knew him since childhood struggled to see the call, destiny and divinity upon his life. They struggled to look beyond his youth and failed to see the greatness within him. If they said this about Jesus, it is likely that people will have similar things to say about you. It is often those who are closest to you who are unable to see extent of God's promises and purpose for your life.

When people know something about your past, they may take it upon themselves to remind you of your past. Satan may try to make you think God cannot use you because of who you used to be or what you used to do. However, with God there is no condemnation to those in Christ Jesus. So, if God has forgiven you and delivered you, then the case is closed. People may try to connect you with things in your past such as past failures or mistakes, but trust and believe in who God says that you are. Do not let anyone put you in a prison of your past experiences. The word to Lot's wife was, "don't look back!" When God delivers you from something, be delivered and don't go back.

Releasing Miracles

What happened when they dishonored Jesus in Matthew 13? There was a drought. "And He did not many mighty works or miracles there because of their unbelief." The flow of miracles ceased in that region, because they did not believe and because they dishonored Jesus. A drought of the flow of miracles ensued. The text says that Jesus did not perform many miracles, signs, wonders, and healings in that place as a result of their dishonor and unbelief. They were cut off and Jesus did not pour out the blessings and miracles of heaven upon them. When you honor God and each other it creates an atmosphere of love where the Spirit of God and miracles can flow.

If you need God to move in your situation, your health, finances, family or even your job then create an atmosphere that will invite Him to come in and move miraculously. Create this atmosphere through honor. Believe God's promises. Honor Him by giving of yourself. Honor Him with your attitude. Honor Him by how you treat others. Honor Him by watching what you say. Honor Him by living a life of holiness and righteousness. Honor Him by living a life of faith and obedience.

The previous chapter, Matthew 12, speaks of the miracles Jesus performed. There was a man with a withered hand and Jesus commanded him to stretch forth his hand.

> "Then saith he to the man, Stretch forth thine hand. And he stretched it forth; and it was restored whole, like as the other. Then the Pharisees went out, and held a council against him, how they might destroy him. When Jesus knew it, he withdrew himself from thence: and great multitudes followed him, and he healed them all," (Matthew 12:13-15 KJV).

The Pharisees were very focused on traditions and religious order and they got offended, because Jesus healed someone on the Sabbath. Verse 14 says they held a meeting about how to destroy Him. Jesus healed a man, the Pharisees got mad and they started plotting about how to kill Him.

What was Jesus' response? He withdrew from that place. Again we see where dishonor abounded God chose not to release blessings and miracles in that place. Dishonor inhibits the flow of miracles. As a result of their dishonor and unbelief, Jesus withdrew Himself from that place. The Pharisees got to talking and showing out and causing a raucous and Jesus got out of there. If Jesus left when people started showing out, shouldn't we do the same? If people around you begin speaking against what God is doing, depart from that place. Do not be associated with dishonor and wrong-doing. You must be careful who you surround yourself with. You may not be the one who is mouthing off or showing dishonor, but the text says that miracles were not performed

in that entire region because of the dishonor and unbelief.

Honoring Parents

The Bible commands you to honor your parents. It does not say honor perfect parents. You are instructed to honor your parents. Honor parents, it is part of the order God instituted, and honoring both natural and spiritual parents brings honor to God. It is easy to honor parents when they treat you well, but what about when they mistreat you?

As difficult as it may be, when you honor a parent who was wronged you it breaks the cycle of dishonor. Believers should not perpetuate ungodly behavior. Do not continue the cycle of dishonor by responding with further dishonor such as talking about them and slandering their name. Instead, God commands that you honor your parents, all parents, not just perfect ones. Honor all parents no matter what mistakes they have made in life. It does not matter how they caused you harm. God's commands that you show them honor. If you mistreat them, you will only perpetuate the cycle.

As difficult as it may be, when you honor a parent who was wronged you it breaks the cycle of dishonor.

Break the cycle and prepare the way for breakthrough to be released in your life by honoring your parents. The Bible tells you to honor your parents (natural and spiritual,) that your days will be long. Spiritual parents can include mentors, teachers, spiritual leaders and more. The Bible gives instruction to honor all parents. When you honor your parents a generational blessing of strength and longevity comes upon your life.

Chapter 16: The Road to Unshakable Faith

Many people claim that they want to be powerfully anointed, but when it comes down to it are you willing to pay the price for the anointing? Abraham was. He left his home, his friends and his place of comfort to follow God. He discovered that answering the call of God requires great faith. It takes faith to venture out of your zone of comfort and familiarity. It takes faith to leave your familiar place and to get on the path that God will show you. Abraham did not know where he was headed. This was not a road he traveled before. God was doing something different with Abraham, taking him in a new direction and it required great faith. Abraham needed to trust God completely. He could not get ahead of God or lag behind Him. Abraham had to remain in God's perfect will and timing in order to fulfill God's perfect plan for him.

When it comes down to it are you willing to pay the price for the anointing?

Hear, See, Know

In 1 Kings 18 we find Elijah on top of Mount Carmel. After three years of drought, Elijah discerned that the season was about to change, the drought had come to an end. Before rain ever showed up, Elijah heard the sound of the rain drawing near. His ear was tuned in to the frequency of heaven. Elijah heard the sound of rain before it arrived, and this should not be considered unusual. He was accustomed to moving in the realm of the miraculous.

Like Ezra, Elijah knew well the voice of God and spent precious time in His presence. Elijah knew how to listen for the sound of heaven and when the sound of the drought ending was released, he heard it first. Amos 3:7 tells us that God does nothing without first revealing it to His servants, the prophets. God speaks to more than those designated as prophets. God speaks to all who will listen! Therefore, we should expect to receive key insight direction and revelation from God concerning the times and seasons and what we are to do in every circumstance.

Stubborn Faith

Elijah crouched down low at the top of Mount Carmel. Everyone else was moving about, but Elijah got down low to the ground. He assumed an even greater place of faith. Elijah heard the sound and he knew what was coming. He did not need to stand up and see the rain to know that rain was coming. Elijah had heard from the Lord, and that was enough for him. He did not have to see it with his natural eyes, instead he looked through the eyes of faith.

Refuse to Be Shaken

Elijah instructed his servant to go and look for the rain. Six times, the servant went and came back with a negative report. "I don't see it," the servant replied six times. Each time Elijah sent the servant back to "look again." It is critical to note that Elijah never shifted from his place of faith. He did not worry or fret. Elijah remained crouched low atop Mount Carmel awaiting the arrival of rain, confirmation that the drought had ended. Even after six times with a negative report, Elijah did not budge from the place of faith, because he knew regardless of what the situation looked like that the drought was over and change had come. He took a firm stance upon the word of the Lord and refused to be moved from that place. Elijah had stubborn faith, resolute faith, and strong faith. Without a doubt in this account Elijah had unshakable faith.

At times you may find yourself feeling like the servant. You may tell the Lord, "I know you said my situation is going to change, but I don't see it. My change still has not come. In fact, the conditions seem to be getting worse."

The instruction to you is, "Look again, look again, and look again. Take another look at the situation. See through the eyes of faith, rather than with your natural vision."

Though Elijah was physically crouching on the mountain, he was standing tall in the realm of the spirit. To stand means to be fixed, unmovable, steadfast, and unshakable. That was the stance Elijah took on the word from the Lord. Elijah's heart was steadfast, unmovable, and unshakable. He had heard from the Lord. Elijah heard the sound of rain being released from heaven. A sound he had not heard in at least three years, but Elijah knew the sound. He was certain that the drought had ended. The servant came back on the sixth time saying "Master, I went and checked six times, there is still nothing there." Elijah did not even lift his head. Elijah was sure. He heard the word, and that caused faith to spring up in his heart. He knew that God was going to do just as he said. Your eyes can deceive you. Do not rely on your eyes. Do not lean to your own understanding. Trust God above all else, and take a firm stance upon His Word and His promises for your life.

Though Elijah was physically crouching on the mountain, he was standing tall in the realm of the spirit.

Oh, that should be our stance! Elijah did not budge from his place of faith. He knew that God would perform just what He said. Elijah just knew. On the seventh time, the servant saw that small cloud approaching, it the first visible sign that the season was changing and rain was coming. However, Elijah did not need to see the cloud, because he was postured in a place of strong faith. Seeing with his natural eyes was not necessary, because he had received the word in his heart and was seeing through the eyes of faith. Elijah heard the sound of rain. He saw the coming rains when others could only see the absence of rain. Elijah knew by faith that the seasons had changed and he responded with appropriate action. Faith should always have corresponding action.

After the tiny cloud appeared Elijah began to run, he ran so fast that he surpassed Ahab's chariot. When God gives you an instruction and His timing springs forth, you should respond accordingly, and run with the vision God has given you. God wants to accelerate you in His will for your life. Acceleration is often released after seasons of delay. There was a three year drought or period of delayed release, but when the drought ended, acceleration was released in the region. You too must anticipate times of acceleration following seasons of delay. If you have been in a season of delay, ask God to release acceleration in your life.

Faith Hears

Romans 10:17 tells us that, "faith cometh by hearing and hearing by the Word of God." Your faith should be quickened and activated every time you hear the Word of God. When you hear or study God's Word it should take root in your heart and causes faith to spring up and bloom.

Faith hears, so be careful to guard your ears. You cannot lend your ears to just anything. Many see no harm in gossip if they themselves are not the one spreading the gossip.

However, the Bible is clear when it comes to evil communications and gossip. "Evil communications corrupt good manners," (1 Corinthians 15:33 NIV). Even if your intentions are good and honorable, you can find yourself becoming tainted by the venom of negative speaking.

"Do not touch God's anointed and do His prophets no harm," (1 Chronicles 16:22). Many fail to realize this and fall into the cycle of touching and slaying people verbally each day. People are verbally annihilated every day. I often call it "murder of the mouth" and it happens far too often in churches and faith communities. Some turn away from the church and their destiny because of the lashings they receive by the tongues of another.

There is a childhood saying *"sticks and stones may break my bones, but words will never harm."* I strongly disagree, words hurt and can be very destructive if used recklessly and abusively. God expects believers to teach, train, and correct others in love, not murder and crucify them verbally. Be so careful of what you say and how you say it. This does not mean you should shy away from giving correction, and requiring that all maintain a high standard and level of accountability, but it does mean that you should do and say everything in love.

Beware Pollution

Faith hears so you must be ever careful of what you listen to and entertain. God did not create your ears to be waste cans. Your ears are directly connected to your heart and when you hear negative speaking such as gossip, lies, complaining, and perverseness it filters in and can pollute your heart and mind. Remember, evil communications lead to corruption. Do not think you can surround yourself with negativity and not be affected.

Fear, doubt and unbelief war directly against your faith. If you are one who often listens to people speaking words of doubt and fear, you can expect that you will battle in the area of your faith. Fear, doubt and unbelief are detrimental to faith. You must believe to obtain eternal salvation and even the promises of God for your life.

The easiest way to know what is in your own heart is to listen to what comes out of your mouth. This is a test I recommend that all people take. For one week, pay close attention to everything that rises in your thoughts and tumbles out of your mouth. Luke 6:45 tells us "out of the abundance of the heart the mouth speaks." That means whatever is abounding in your heart is going to come out of your mouth. That's the Word. If doubt and unbelief are abounding in your heart, that is what will come out of your mouth. If lust is abounding in your heart, it will be evidenced in your thoughts and your conversations. Your confession originates in your heart. I challenge you to try that exercise and see what is abounding in your own heart.

The easiest way to know what is in your own heart is to listen to what comes out of your mouth.

The Eyes of Faith

God showed Abraham a powerful vision in Genesis 13:14-15. "Now lift up your eyes and look from the place where you are, north, east, south and west, for all the land which you see, I will give it to you and to your descendants forever." What a promise! God told Abraham to lift up his eyes and look from the place where he was to all of the places God was showing him. This is a tremendous key to strong faith.

In essence God was saying, "Abraham, do not let your eyes settle on where you are right now. Do not get stuck at what your situation and surroundings look like right now. Lift up your eyes and look to the north, east, south and west and see through the eyes of faith."

Do not get stuck looking at the difficulty of your present circumstances or you may fail to see the good that is on the horizon. There is more that God wants to show you. Lift up your eyes from the place where you are, and see the greater picture for your life. It stretches across the north, east, south and west of you. The place where you are right now is not your end result. There is much more God desires to do through you. At that moment Abraham could not physically see all that God was promising him. God was encouraging Abraham to see and lay hold of it through the avenue of faith.

You step into the arena of unshakable faith when you begin to see through the eyes of faith, and are not moved by the appearance of a situation. Regardless of what it looks like you continue to stand in faith. Unshakable faith leads you to look for God in every situation and take your stand upon His word and promises. Unshakable faith refuses to compromise and refuses to quit. A person with unshakable faith is not

Standing on the Promises

distracted or worried by storms raging, their focus remains on God and what He said about the matter. They know that man's "no" cannot compare to God's "yes." A person with unshakable faith knows that God has the final say!

Unshakable faith leads you to look for God in every situation and take your stand upon His word and promises.

My prayer partner, Taiwan Brown, has a saying that is powerfully true. She often declares, "Christina, people have it wrong. Many think that seeing is believing, but in actuality believing is seeing."

Let me explain. We should not believe something because we can see it. We must believe even when we do not see it. Our faith must not be predicated upon whether or not we can see what God has spoken, or what we are working towards and hoping for. Our faith should be predicated upon the Word of God and what He has spoken concerning our lives. We walk by faith and not by sight (2 Corinthians 5:7). Instead of seeing through natural physical eyes we should see through the eyes of faith. Do not focus on what it looks like in the natural. Focus on what God has said and stand on the infallible truth of His word, it cannot fail.

My prayer partner, Taiwan Brown, has a saying that is powerfully true. She often declares, "Christina, people have it wrong. Many think that seeing is believing, but in actuality believing is seeing."

Faith Speaks

"You will also decree a thing and it shall be established: and light will shine upon your ways." (Job 22:28). When you operate in faith you are rightly positioned to speak in agreement with heaven. This is a powerful weapon. There is tremendous power in your words and speaking in agreement with God. Every single time you open your mouth, you can either speak in agreement with heaven or hell. Who have you been partnering with?

Some people frequently utter words such as "I'm sick and tired. I never have any money. I just want to give up. I just can't succeed at this." When statements like these leave your mouth, you are partnering with hell and giving fuel and instruction to the forces of darkness. Satan capitalizes on the words of weary believers every day! You cannot afford to let just anything come out of your mouth. There is great power in your words. Use them wisely. What does God say about the matter? Who does He say that you are? I know you may not feel blessed at the moment, but what promises has God spoken in His Word that apply to your life? When you speak in agreement with God's Word and with His promises, His glorious power is released in your situation.

Satan capitalizes on the words of weary believers every day!

If you are not speaking towards your good, you very well may be speaking your demise. The choice is yours. When you speak negatively and complain you are partnering with hell. Job 22:28 tells us that we can decree a thing and it shall be established. It will be established. This includes the good things you speak, but it also includes the bad things that leave your mouth. If you decree that you are always broke, sick and tired. Then you can anticipate remaining in a state of being broke, sick and tired.

Consider Galatians 6:7-8, "Be not deceived, God is not mocked. Whatsoever a man soweth that shall he also reap." When you speak words, you are sowing seed with your mouth. Galatians 6:8 says you will reap what you sow. What are you sowing with your mouth? Are you speaking words of faith, life, blessing and truth? Or are you complaining, gossiping and tearing down others with your words? The Word of God is true. What you sow is what you shall reap. It is foolish to sow words of death and destruction, and then look for a harvest of blessing and life. That is contrary to the principles of God's Word and it will not produce the harvest you desire. If you want to see a harvest of life, blessing, favor and productivity spring up in your life, you must sow accordingly with your words. Speak words of life, encouragement, kindness and blessing to and about others. Let good things come out of your mouth and watch the harvest that springs forth.

Chapter 17: Don't Give Up

One sunny day in 2007, a stranger walked up to me and handed me a slip of paper. On that paper was a simple message that greatly challenged my faith. The paper read, "Objects in mirror are closer than they appear." I knew this to be the familiar phrase, which is printed on car mirrors throughout the world. As I sought the Lord for the meaning of this unusual message, the Holy Spirit impressed upon me the need to go to a mirror.

I went to the bathroom mirror and saw my familiar reflection. Nothing had changed. No sudden weight loss or brilliant glory rested upon me. Same outdated hairstyle, same features, no changes were evident. As I stood there looking deeply into the mirror, I heard those words resonate in my heart. I looked at that piece of paper quite puzzled. The words had my attention, but their meaning escaped me.

Again, I read the words, "Objects in mirror are closer than they appear." I began to mumble those words aloud, seeking to grasp their meaning for my life. Something started to make sense within my heart. I began to speak those words aloud with certainty, as they fully came alive within me. Suddenly, I was shouting with great faith *"Yes, the objects in mirror are closer than they appear!"*

What does that mean? What objects in the mirror? Stand in front of a mirror, my friend. The object in the mirror is you! You are closer to your destination that it may seem or appear! Let that resonate in your heart. The objects in the mirror are those things concerning you that have yet to show up in fullness. Your vision, dreams, hopes and desires that burn in your heart. All these things are closer than they appear. Grab ahold of that. The things you have been looking for and waiting on are closer than they may appear! Those things that you have been pursuing are closer than it seems. Your goals, your business success, and the fulfillment of your dreams are all closer than they appear.

It seemed that my hopes and dreams had died, and withered to nothing more than a distant memory.

As I reflected on these words, tears streamed down my face. You can tell by now that a message from God is sure to leave me in tears! This was a word I needed to hear desperately. I was in a season where doubt and weariness were knocking at my door with a battering ram! In that season I focused so heavily on my problems that I had lost sight of God's promises. I was overwhelmed by the tests and trials that abounded in my life. Many days I felt like I was drowning, and it took all I had to stay afloat. It seemed that my hopes and dreams had died, and withered to nothing more than a distant memory. Then I received that timely revelation from the heart of God. God is so faithful! A perfect stranger handed me a slip of paper with the words, "Objects in mirror are closer than they appear." That let me know that God had not forgotten about me and in fact He was well aware of my circumstance. He saw my pain and sent me a special message to encourage my heart to not give up (Galatians 6:9). Objects in mirror are closer than they may appear. I believe that is a word for you as well! Those things that the Lord has spoken and promised you are closer than they may appear!

I realized that my destiny and the things God had spoken to my heart and promised me were closer than I ever imagined. As that heavy weight of deferred hope lifted off me, I did something that some may think quite strange. I lifted my hands in worship unto the Lord. You must understand that God's ways are not our ways or His thoughts our thoughts (Isaiah 55:8). The weight of weariness was beginning to lift, but it was not totally gone. When I lifted my hands in worship, it was as though heaven's gates opened above me and a stream of God's perfect love was poured out upon me. It surrounded me like a warm blanket. Tears streamed down my face as the heavy weights fell from my life. To my amazement I began to do something I had not done in months. I began to laugh. Not your typical ha-ha he-he laugh. This was a deep soulful laugh. It seemed that my entire being was laughing as an unspeakable joy welled up within me. This joy was new. Like nothing I had experienced before. I remembered that in the Lord we find fullness of joy!

That laughter was a sure sign of joy and hope being restored in my life. It was glorious and lifted me out of that ugly pit of despair where I had been held captive. Suddenly, a Scripture welled up in my heart. "The joy of the Lord is your strength," (Nehemiah 8:10 NIV).

Rejoice beloved! The joy of the Lord is your strength. No matter what the situation looks like, the joy of the Lord is your strength. When you are in the midst of trials and hardships and your joy seems deficient, look to God and reflect on His goodness, therein you will find joy. Through the joy of the Lord, God imparts strength. The joy He gives far exceeds any earthly joy or pleasure. It is beyond comparison.

Right now I want to pray for God to impart a fresh measure of joy into your life. In fact, I encourage you to lift up your hands and declare that the objects in your mirror are closer than they appear. It may seem like the fulfillment of your hopes and dreams is still far away. You may not even be able to see how they could possibly come to past, but take heart, objects in mirror are closer than they appear! Your breakthrough is closer. Your deliverance is closer. Your hopes and dreams are closer than they may appear! Trust God and do not doubt. I invite you to pray the following prayer with me.

Personal Prayer

Father God, I rejoice now. Even in the midst of trials and obstacles, I rejoice and give you praise and thanks. I ask you to set me free from the bondages of doubt and despair. Strengthen me and help me to overcome weariness. Remove every heavy weight from my life. Cause a shift in the atmosphere around me. Now

Lord I ask you to impart joy to my heart. I want to experience fullness of joy. Cause joy to arise in me. You promised to give me the oil of joy for mourning. I decree that the season of mourning is over, and joy is here. The joy of the Lord is my strength! In Jesus Name, Amen. Now, receive it and give God thanks.

Overcoming Procrastination

What has God called you to begin that you are still dragging your feet about? What has been brewing in your heart that you have not begun? In the pursuit of your purpose, you must expose and overcome obstacles such as distractions, fear, rejection and doubt. One of the biggest nemeses to success and moving forward is procrastination, and it must be overcome. In a society where busyness and working excessively is a hallmark, it is easy to fall into the pattern of being busy, doing too much, and failing to focus on your God-given purpose. Procrastination can easily cause your process to be prolonged.

For years I was the, "queen of excuses." I could have easily earned a graduate level college degree in "excuses." I had an excuse for everything. I knew what I should have been doing, but found many solid reasons as to why I could not do it at the time. Excuses were consuming my future and destiny like vicious termites in a lumber yard, and that's putting it mildly. Procrastination can consume your time, hopes, dreams, motivation and much more if you allow it. If you are not careful, excuses can push you farther and farther away from the very place God has planned for you to thrive. It has been well said that it is easier to put off until tomorrow, or the next day, or the next week what you can do today, but oftentimes that is not profitable or beneficial to your progress and success.

One of the biggest nemeses to success and moving forward is procrastination, and it must be overcome.

Calculated effort, discipline and diligence are needed to subdue this procrastination giant. When you make a calculated decision to obey God's voice at every interval of your life's journey, you will find success in overcoming the procrastination foe. Giving in to procrastination and slothfulness can cause you to miss out on God's timing and His will for your life. People who habitually procrastinate become notorious for delaying, missing opportunities and even remaining in a place of spiritual stagnation. God has called you to do the precise opposite. Go forward in your purpose, obey God's leading and direction, do things today and do not make excuses or empty justifications. If you find yourself in a rut, and cannot seem to figure out how you got into the rut, or how to break free from it, give yourself a self-assessment. Excessive excuses and procrastination could be the reason you are there and cause for your delay.

No More Procrastination

Procrastination can be deadly. Many procrastinate with their spirituality. Many delay and procrastinate about accepting Christ as their Lord and Savior. Some claim that they are waiting for the right time, others note that if they accept Christ now they will have to give up certain pleasures they find enjoyable. So, the procrastination swells and grows, engulfing them. It is a race against the clock. A dangerous game they are playing. The Lord desires that all be saved and none perish, but the decision is yours. Sadly for some, procrastination may cause them to miss out on spending eternity in heaven.

It is time to break free from the clutches of self-delay and procrastination and walk fully in the obedience of God. Discover His plan for your life and walk in it. Obedience to God takes precedence. When the Lord speaks to you and tells you to do something, do it. Walk by faith and not by sight. Do not procrastinate for years until what God is requiring of you seems more palatable. Live a life of obedience to God and procrastination will evaporate from your life. What is the Lord telling you to do today?

Chapter 18: Finding the Pavilion of God

There is protection in the presence of God. In Psalm chapter 27 we find David telling of a battle he faced. It is no secret that David was a highly skilled leader and warrior. From the frontlines of battle, to going toe-to-toe with Goliath, David was an expert in the art of war. As a shepherd boy, he overpowered a bear and lion with his own hands. David even sent demons flying when he played his harp strings. David was a valiant leader and fighter, highly skilled in the art of war. He led many men into battle and conquered many opposing armies. He knew when to engage in hand to hand combat and when to draw the line. In today's vernacular he might be considered a great general or a war strategist because of his high level of experience and expertise. So, in Psalm chapter 27 we see David employing a new strategy that confounded his enemies.

A Place of Protection

When David's enemies rose to devour his flesh, even when he was greatly outnumbered, he did not fear. Instead David sought refuge in the pavilion of God. David knew that no matter what his enemies did or how they advanced against him that he had a shield, a strong tower, a fortress of defense that surpassed the strength and might of any earthly army.

"For in the time of trouble He shall hide me in His pavilion: in the secret of His tabernacle shall he hide me; He shall set me up upon a rock," (Psalm 27:5 NIV). David sought safety in the pavilion of God.

Part of David's great success when facing an enemy was his understanding of God's ways. David understood that things are not always as they appear. One looking at a boy facing a great nine foot Philistine giant would think surely this boy will be destroyed, but David knew that He did not fight alone. David also understood that things are not always as they seem. David understood that retreating into the presence of God, was actually an offensive maneuver. That may seem strange, because many think of retreating as running away scared when someone is outnumbered, fleeing for their life. That is how many commonly think of retreating, but I submit to you that retreating is actually a power move, that will put the enemy at bay and position you to receive the promises of God. When was the last time you retreated into the presence of God?

One looking at a boy facing a great nine foot Philistine giant would think surely this boy will be destroyed, but David knew that He did not fight alone.

Battles will go in your favor simply because you recognize the power of your position and employ the kingdom strategy of retreating into God. David understood that even in his retreating, he was still advancing against the enemy, and he did not lose any ground.

Let's look at another definition of retreat, which will help us gain a better understanding of how this is an offensive maneuver. To retreat can also mean to purposefully enter into a place of rest, seclusion or safety. This definition of retreat speaks of advancing, that is a far cry from running away scared. We see here that retreat can also imply that one is moving forward with calculation and purpose.

Battles will go in your favor simply because you recognize the power of your position and employ the kingdom strategy of retreating into God.

Standing on the Promises

    I believe that when David wrote Psalm chapter 27, he was recalling a time when the enemy had him surrounded and it seemed all hope was lost. His camp was surrounded and outnumbered. The enemy was encroaching upon his territory. No matter which way David turned, trouble was there, ready to pounce on him and devour his flesh. When it seemed like it was over and the enemy was about to overtake him, I believe that David opened up his mouth and released a war cry from his belly. Not just any cry, but I believe David began to call on Jehovah. Proverbs 18:10 tells us that "the name of the Lord is a strong tower." The very name of the Lord is a strong tower. So when David called upon the name of the Lord, the strong tower of God opened unto him and he was able to step into that place of safety and refuge. Proverbs 18:10 also says the righteous run into it and they are safe. To his enemies it may have looked like David was scared and running away. It may have looked like David was giving up, but in actuality David was running with purpose. He was running into the refuge of the Lord. David understood that God was his refuge and strength, a present help in the time of trouble.

A Place of Peace

    David knew that he could not stay where he was. The enemy had infiltrated his camp and was closing in on him. I believe David recognized that there was benefit in getting out of that place of oppression and into the pavilion of God. There was benefit in his retreating to God. I don't know what your situation looks like, if the enemy has you surrounded and is closing in on you? Does it seem that you are surrounded on all sides by struggles, marital and relationship issues, financial issues and health concerns? It may seem like you are outnumbered and pressed on every side, but be reminded of David. He was surrounded on every side by an army of opposition, but David knew that if he could just make it to the pavilion of God that everything would be alright.

    I believe David had to press past some situations and obstacles to get there. I believe he even had to cut some people loose who were not willing to go with him. David had to step over some people who only wanted to talk about him and stand in his way. David had to leave some people behind. I believe David may have even had to cry some tears, but he knew that if he could just make it to the pavilion of God that everything would be alright. The pavilion of God is a place where God's presence dwells.

> "We are hard pressed on every side, but not crushed; perplexed, but not in despair; persecuted, but not abandoned; struck down, but not destroyed." (2 Corinthians 4:8-9 NIV). What a powerful passage of Scripture. It is filled with tremendous hope. This passage reveals that trouble may come, but that does not mean you are defeated. You can be pressed on every side, but not crushed. You can be perplexed, but not in despair. You can be struck down, but that does not mean you are destroyed. There is always hope! Never stop hoping and believing. Refuse to succumb to the trouble that may arise in your life. Take a firm stand with hope and faith as your constant companions.

The Key of Daniel

When the decree went out that all must bow down to the King or else be thrown into the den of lions, Daniel's actions did not change (Daniel 6). Daniel continued to pray to the one true God. He did not hide his love and devotion to God. He prayed and worshipped in front of an open window in his upper room. Daniel was charged with defying the King's decree. As a result, Daniel was thrown into the den of lions.

It is critical to note that when Daniel was thrown into the den of lion's, he already had an established relationship with God. Daniel knew that God was with him and I believe that even before his feet touched the floor of that den, Daniel had already had a conversation with God. Daniel knew that angels had been dispatched to bind up the mouths of the lions. So, Daniel entered the den in peace. Imagine that, being thrown into a den of ravenous lions in perfect peace! That is the power of God in action.

You may be in a den of lion's situation right now. Be careful how you react. The natural response when the heat is turned up is to be afraid and

Standing on the Promises

discouraged, but Daniel's victory was in His ability to trust God completely and hear God's instruction. I believe Daniel heard the Lord say, "I sent my angels to bind up the mouths of the lions." Daniel still had to face those lions, but he did not have to fight them! You can spend so much time worrying and crying about your situation that you miss your supernatural victory! It is easy to become so stressed and overwhelmed by the appearance of your circumstance, that you find yourself wrestling with an enemy who has already been defeated! Daniel could have wrestled with those paralyzed lions all night long, but he heard God and knew that they were already defeated. You must be careful not to become so stressed out and overwhelmed that you miss God. Daniel could have wasted much time, strength and effort unnecessarily.

Daniel still had to face those lions, but he did not have to fight them!

Daniel understood that as long as he was in the presence of the Lord that he was safe. So instead of fighting, Daniel entered the pavilion of the Lord and rested in peace, despite what the situation may have looked like. You too can go through life in perfect peace. Daniel knew and trusted God completely. As a result, Daniel turned right to God when he needed help and guidance. Daniel rested in the pavilion of God. He found constant peace in the Lord's presence. Your peace should not be predicated upon what is going on around you. Your peace should always remain, no matter the circumstances or obstacles.

Peace is a byproduct of unshakable faith. When you have entered a place of unshakable faith, you can look trouble in the face and remain in a place of perfect peace. Just like David when he faced that great Philistine giant. David said it best when he declared to his adversary, I don't come in my own name, "I come in the name of the Lord," (1 Samuel 17:45 NKJV).

Peace is a by product of unshakable faith.

"Peace I leave with you; my peace I give you. I do not give to you as the world gives. Do not let your hearts be troubled and do not be afraid," (John

14:27 NIV). When you stand in faith and in agreement with the will of God, you have the backing of heaven. Continue to stand. Stand in faith and watch peace flood your situation

Chapter 19: Your Waiting is not in Vain

Many can relate to the man in John chapter 5. He was in a severe season of waiting. He had been sick for thirty-eight years. He was positioned in close proximity to the pool of Bethesda for an extended number of years. He was waiting for someone to intervene on his behalf and help him into the pool. He was waiting for something to happen in his favor.

I know what it feels like to wait. I was recently in a season of waiting in my life. I was seeking God for direction and I was determined to be still and wait on God. I read my Bible, prayed, and stood in faith. I was waiting on God to move in my life. In essence, I was waiting for the stirring of the waters like the man in John chapter 5. I was waiting for God to show up mightily and move in my life. I waited and waited. Spent time in deep prayer and kept on waiting. I was waiting on God to move. Finally, the Lord spoke to my heart and what He said was not at all what I expected.

The Lord said to me, "Christina, what are you waiting for?"

I thought that sure is a strange question. I gave a confident reply, "Um, I'm waiting on You."

And He answered with the greatest of care and conviction, "I am with you Christina, and I am waiting on you to move."

Here I was thinking that I was waiting on a miraculous stirring of the waters. I was waiting on God to part the heavens and show up mightily bringing change to my situation, but in actuality He was there all along and He was waiting on me to move. I had been waiting and waiting on God, and all that time He was waiting on me. How often does this happen in our lives? Have you been waiting on God, when in actuality He is waiting on you?

Have you been waiting past your season of waiting?

There are definite seasons of waiting which may seem like a delay, holding pattern or even like a wilderness experience. Definite seasons of waiting, but if you are not careful you can miss when your season changes. Just as sure as spring changes into summer and fall changes into winter, life seasons change. Did your season of waiting end and a new season start without your knowledge? Have you been waiting past your season of waiting?

Delay is Not Denial

Your delay was not a denial. Take up your bed and walk. Rise from the place where you have been stuck. Move from the place where you have been drifting. Rise from your resting place. Rise from the bed of hurt, resentment and affliction. The Lord desires to bind up your wounds and broken heart so that you can move forward into your purpose and destiny. The Lord thy God is with you and He is faithful and will deliver you out of your place of pain and hurt. As you press in to Him, you will experience His immeasurably great love. He will bind up your broken heart and bring healing and restoration to every disappointment. God is calling you forward. An open door stands before you Will you go through it? Exodus 4:12 speaks of a season of going where God is calling you to go. It says, "Now go and the Lord thy God will be with you and shall tell you what to say and do." Know that as you go forward that God is with you and will guide and direct your pathway.

I am reminded of 2 Timothy 1:6 which says "I remind you to stir up the gift of God, which is in you." Stir up the gift, which is in you. The gifts you need to succeed are already within you. There is greatness within you, and God can use you to fulfill His plans and purposes in the earth. Far too often, when it comes to gifts and anointing, people look everywhere, but inside themselves, much like the man in John chapter 5.

When Jesus approached him and asked him if he was ready to be made whole, he hesitated and gave Jesus excuses. "But they won't help me, and when

I try to make it to the pool, others keep passing me. I can't do it." Instead of being full of faith, he was full of excuses.

God wants you to be whole. He wants your marriage to be whole, nothing lacking. He wants to fill every void in your life.

God is not asking for excuses, He is asking, "Will you be made whole?" Wholeness speaks of moving from a place of incompleteness to a state of completeness through the process of divine restoration. God wants you to be whole. He wants your marriage to be whole, nothing lacking. He wants to fill every void in your life. God wants to restore life to the weary and wholeness to the broken. Will you be made whole?

Over the Rainbow

Some weeks ago I was driving home from work and I saw a spectacular sight. I saw a rainbow stretching across the sky. This rainbow was so breathtaking it looked like it stretched right out of heaven and was masterfully painted across the sky. I began to remember in Genesis chapter 9 when the Lord gave the rainbow after the flood as a sign of His covenant promise that He would never again destroy the earth by water. The rainbow is a sign of God's promises extended to you. Just as a rainbow seems to stretch out of heaven and reach the earth, in like manner are the promises of God for your life. They originate from God and extend right to you. There are promises with your name on them. Always remember, what God has for you is for you. Do not forfeit your blessings. Receive all that God has for you.

I reflected on that as I gazed at the brilliant rainbow. I heard the Lord speak to my heart, "many people cannot see their rainbow because of the clouds and rain in their life."

Have you lost sight of what God has promised you, because your focus is on the rain instead of the rainbow? Has the heaviness of your circumstance consumed you and obscured your vision? What has God placed in your heart? What has He spoken concerning you? You must remember that the rainbow is supposed to be a reminder that the rain in your life will not destroy you. The rainbow is a reminder that your promise is certain, and that the elements in your life will not overtake you. Your promise is sure.

"Many people cannot see their rainbow because of the clouds and rain in their life."

The man in John chapter 5 was sitting in walking distance from his promise. Imagine that! He was in walking distance of the very thing that would transform his life! He had been sick for thirty-eight years, and his healing was just steps away. Wholeness and completeness was within reach. His promise was close enough that he could walk to it.

I believe that many of you are just as close to what God has promised you. Let me remind you that a promise is a promise. Your heart's desires, hopes and dreams God has not forgotten. Do not grow weary in your well doing, do not grow weary in your waiting, do not grow weary as you trust God and walk by faith. Your due season is approaching and you shall reap. This is not the time to give up on your hopes and dreams. This is not the time to lose sight of what God has promised you.

Jesus spoke to the man at the pool and his entire situation changed in an instant. After thirty-eight years, five words changed his life forever. In actuality, one word from the Lord can change your life forever. Never underestimate the power of the word of God. All it takes is one word from God and every obstacle in your life must yield.

When it comes to waiting, my golden rule is, "Worship while you wait."

There is a tendency to wither under the pressures and disappointments of waiting. Yet, this must not happen. Do not wither and do not grow weary. Press your way through and continue to worship, continue to pray and believe God, and continue to live by faith as you trust God for the fulfillment of your hopes, dreams and purpose. Bloom where you are planted and refuse to wither and quit. Even when circumstances seem oppressive and overwhelming, put your hope in God and continue to believe. Be faithful to God while you wait. There is an old saying that says, "Whistle while you work."

When it comes to waiting, my golden rule is, "Worship while you wait." Worship and praise are powerful weapons. I will cover this further in the next chapter.

Chapter 20: Another Dimension of Blessing

"And when they had laid many stripes upon them, they cast them into prison, charging the jailor to keep them safely: Who, having received such a charge, thrust them into the inner prison, and made their feet fast in the stocks. At midnight Paul and Silas prayed, and sang praises unto God: and the prisoners heard them. Suddenly there was a great earthquake, so that the foundations of the prison were shaken: and immediately all the doors were opened, and every one's bands were loosed," (Acts 16:23-26 KJV).

This Bible account begins with the arrest of Paul and Silas. The local Philippian authorities beat them and unjustly threw them into prison. Besides the trauma of the severe beating, their legs were fastened in stocks, which likely caused great discomfort and limited their mobility. According to the standards of that day, a prison closely resembled a dungeon, a dark frightening place with no facility for waste or comforts of any kind.

In spite of the savage conditions, unjust imprisonment and pain in their bodies Paul and Silas did not succumb to their circumstances or environment. They could have easily become depressed, fearful and hopeless. In fact one may expect such a response, but Paul and Silas were able to transcend their surroundings and tap into the presence of God.

As the story goes, a sound was heard round about midnight. Paul and Silas were heard praying and singing praises to God! What a strange sound this must have been to the other prisoners who were used to hearing the crying, groaning and complaining of their fellow beaten and chained prisoners. Yet, a different sound permeated the darkness. It was a sound of joy and faith, a sound that caused hope to rise in the hearts of the prisoners. As Paul and Silas sang songs and praises to God in the midst of the prison, something happened. The Bible says that suddenly, there was an earthquake that shook the prison! The doors flung open, and the shackles of Paul, Silas and every other prisoner were released! This reveals a powerful key of blessing. Praise and worship beckons the King of Glory!

Paul and Silas were men of faith who knew how to elevate their hearts above their trials and circumstances and enter the glory, presence and power of God. Through praise and worship their hearts transcended the reality of that jail cell, and entered the joyous presence and peace of God, opening up the way for God's power to be released in their situation. As they praised in the midnight hour, the angel of the Lord showed up and broke open the prison gates.

Midnight Breakthrough

The Bible says they were singing songs around midnight. You may have heard people say that change often comes "in the midnight hour." Why is that? I believe one reason is due to the prophetic significance of midnight. See, at 11:59 p.m. one day ends, and at midnight a new day begins. Midnight is the point, which represents a shift from the night season to morning. The Bible shares that weeping may endure for a night, but joy comes in the morning. Have you been in a night season where it seems like morning will never come? The night season will not last always. Remember Paul and Silas, and begin to rejoice in your place of pain and testing. Midnight will surely come. A new day is dawning in your life. Get ready to transition from your night season into a new day.

As a result of their praises, Paul and Silas were set free, and so were all of the other prisoners. Two men began to sing and praise God and the entire prison got delivered. All of the captives were set free, because Paul and Silas refused to give up hope and give in to the reality of their situation. Sure, they were in a prison, but they refused to be bound! That should be your confession as well. Refuse to be bound by your circumstances.

The Power of Praise

The Bible says that God inhabits the praises of His people (Psalms 22:3). Praise ushers us out of our circumstances and into the Lord's presence! Praise beckons the Lord to come inhabit the atmosphere that we have established with our words and worship. Praise invites the Lord to come and sit or be enthroned in our praise. When praise is released from your mouth, it beckons the Lord. On the other hand, when complaining, worry and fear are released from our mouths it counters that atmosphere of praise. No matter what your situation looks like, rejoice in the Lord and give Him praise. Praise is the glorious invitation for God to come and inhabit your situation!

Through praise you can transcend places of pain, grief, fear, and depression and enter the peace, joy, and healing presence of God. Praise is a "gate-pass" which allows you to enter the realm of God's glory and unlimited provision.

The psalmist wrote, "Enter into his gates with thanksgiving, and into his courts with praise: be thankful unto him, and bless his name," (Psalms 100:4 KJV). Rejoice today and render praise to God for who He is, not only for what He has done for you. The reason for your praise is not "stuff" or blessings received. The reason for your praise is God! Praise and worship flow out of a heart that is enthralled by the love of God.

Praise is the glorious invitation for God to come and inhabit your situation!

Praise should not be reserved as the thank-you to God when He dispenses goodness. For many that is the extent of their praise and thankfulness to God, giving thanks for a blessing received or prayer answered such as a promotion, new house, financial blessing and the like. Those are good things and they are praiseworthy, but praise was not designed to be rendered exclusively at the receipt of a blessing. The Bible instructs us to render praise at all times (Psalm 34:1). Therefore, no matter what state we are in, whether we are going into a trial or coming out of one, praise is appropriate and desired by God.

David said "I will bless the Lord at all times, and His praise shall continually be in my mouth," (Psalm 34:1 NKJV). David blessed the Lord at all times, not only in the good or prosperous times. David said "I bless the Lord at all times." We should also bless the Lord often, daily, at all times!

Lift up the King of Kings through praise and worship, it invokes His presence and power to flow in your midst. When the praises go up, God Himself comes down (Psalm 22:3). How incredible! Praise delivers a royal invitation for the King of glory to come in!

When the praises go up, God Himself comes down (Psalm 22:3).

However, praise and worship should not only be reserved for Sunday mornings. It should be a consistent part of your lifestyle, much like prayer and fasting. Invite the presence of God in your life daily at work, in the car, at home, in bed or wherever you are. God is worthy of your praise. Offer generous praise to the Lord. Your praise brings the refreshing of the Lord's presence, along with His power and anointing.

The Beauty of Pure Praise

Praise that flows from a pure heart is a sure way to shift the atmosphere. If the atmosphere and circumstances in your life are in need of a change, open up your mouth and release a shout or song of praise! As you sing to the Lord in praise and thankfulness, the presence and glory of the Lord will be invited in, and everything that is unlike God must flee.

Some people are deterred, because they have a preconceived notion of what praise must look like. Various actions can be involved with praise to God, some loud, some quiet, some even silent such as lifting up hands to God or dancing before the Lord. Praise can involve verbal expressions of adoration and thanksgiving, singing, playing instruments, shouting, dancing or clapping your hands. These are only a small portion of the many ways you can render praise to God. However, you must be careful not to focus solely on the actions. True praise is not engaging in these demonstrative actions alone. True praise is birthed in the heart and flows out of a deep love and appreciation for God. When your heart is pure and filled with adoration, praise will pour out of you effortlessly.

Jesus spoke about the hypocrisy of the Pharisees whose worship was only an outward show and not from the heart. "This people draweth nigh unto me with their mouth, and honoureth me with their lips; but their heart is far from me," (Matthew 15:8 KJV).

Genuine praise to God is a matter of humility and sincere devotion to the Lord, and it is rendered in spirit and in truth (John 4:23). Remember, true praise originates in your heart and flows out of a deep love and appreciation for God. Won't you join me in praising Him today? Praise should be how we enter and endure every situation, for it is praise that elevates us above our trials and into the presence of the Lord. Praise invites Him to inhabit our situations fully.

True praise is birthed in the heart and flows out of a deep love and appreciation for God.

Praise and worship should be part of your lifestyle just as healthy eating, strategic planning or prayer and fasting can be part of your lifestyle. Invoke the presence of God in your daily life by spending time developing an atmosphere of praise like Paul and Silas. At work, in the car, at home or anywhere praise to the Lord brings the refreshing of the Lord's presence, along with His power and anointing. Singing songs of praise is an easy way to invite the presence of the Lord, and a sure way to shift atmospheres.

Paul and Silas were in prison unjustly after being severely beaten. That was the reality of their circumstance and yet there was praise in their hearts that rose above their trials and shifted the very atmosphere. The very earth began to quake as God came and inhabited their praises! That's the kind of move of God many of us need in our lives! Bless the Lord at all times and continually fill your mouth with praise.

Through praise we humble ourselves and center our attention upon the Lord with heart-felt expressions of love, adoration and thanksgiving. Praise brings our spirit into a pinnacle of fellowship and intimacy between ourselves and God. It enlightens us and causes us to be keenly aware of our spiritual connection and union with God. Praise transports us into the realm of the supernatural and into the power of God. "Blessed is the people that know the joyful sound: they shall walk, O Lord, in the light of thy countenance," (Psalms 89:15 NKJV).

Praise is an expression of faith and a declaration of victory!

The Lord delights in the love and devotion of His children. Sincere praise pleases the Lord and invites Him to come and dwell where praise is rendered. Praise is an expression of faith and a declaration of victory! It declares that we believe God is with us and is in control of the outcome of all our circumstances. Praise is a "sacrifice," something that we offer to God sacrificially, not just because we feel like it but, because we believe in Him and He is worthy. Praise to God is rendered, because we were created to bring Him glory!

"By him therefore let us offer the sacrifice of praise to God continually, that is, the fruit of our lips giving thanks to his name," (Hebrews 13:15 NKJV).

Praise Sends the Enemy Running

Praise causes the presence of God to show up. You must also realize that praise repels the presence of the enemy. An atmosphere that is filled with sincere worship and praise to God, by humble and contrite hearts, is repulsive to Satan. He fears the power in the name of Jesus, and flees from the Lord's habitation of praise.

Standing on the Promises

When the children of Judah found themselves outnumbered by the hostile armies of Ammon, Moab, and mount Seir, King Jehoshaphat and all the people sought the Lord for divine intervention. The Lord assured the people that this would be His battle. The Lord told them to go out against their enemies, and He would fight for them. So, what did the children of Judah do? They were of the tribe of Judah (Judah actually means praise), and they had enough faith to obey God, even when what He told them to do seemed unusual. In obedience to God, the army called for the praisers! King Jehoshaphat, sent the army of Judah against their enemies, led by the frontline praisers!

On they went, ahead of the army declaring, "Praise the Lord, for His mercy endureth forever!" And the scripture says, "When they began to sing and to praise, the Lord set ambushments against the children of Ammon, Moab, and mount Seir, which were come against Judah; and they were smitten," (2 Chronicles 20:22 KJV).

The only weapon they lifted was the weapon of praise! Praise is powerful and must not be overlooked or undervalued. When God's people begin to praise His name, it sends the enemy running and it causes confusion in his camp. I challenge you to become a person of praise. Expect to experience a release of the power of God in your life!

Personal Prayer

Dear Lord, thank you for Your love and grace. Thank you for taking care of me and my family in every situation. Lord, I ask You to help me release myself to praise and worship You freely. Where the Spirit of the Lord is, there is liberty. Help me to walk in liberty as I praise and worship you at all times. Help me to rise above every adversity and trial. Help me to praise you in spirit and truth. Help me to move past feelings of discomfort and release myself in genuine praise and worship. Inhabit my praise, God! Thank You always. In Jesus Name. Amen.

Chapter 21: Birthing Your Promise

Don't ask me how I knew, I just knew. I woke on Monday April 19, 2010 and knew it was the day I had been waiting for. I knew this was the day our second daughter would be born. The day began with an air of excitement and expectancy. I was not in full blown labor, though I had some sporadic contractions over the past week. My water had not broken and I was not feeling the tell-tale pressure of impending labor, but somehow deep within my heart, I knew the time had finally come. The hurry up and wait game would soon be over. At times that is how it happens with birthing your promise. You may have a knowing that it is time for whatever you have been carrying in your heart to come forth, much like a pregnancy due date.

Ironically, my baby was not due for another three weeks, but I knew the day had arrived. I made the admiral decision not to go to work, especially since I did not want to experience going into labor at work, as I did with our first child.

My husband, Tony, was home. He had taken off the past few weeks from truck driving, to be close to home and help with our three year old, as my belly seemed to grow leaps and bounds by the day. Tony was committed to being at my side during the labor and delivery process, so the long distance driving was temporarily put on hold.

That morning I sat up in bed, looked at Tony and emphatically declared, "Today is the day! Finally, this is it! Now, let's go to Target."

I am sure he thought to himself, "It is official, my wife has lost it." Of course this was not the first time he wondered this about me. So, he bravely asked the question that was nagging at his mind, "Honey, why exactly do we need to go to Target?"

I rolled out of bed, which took a great amount of grunting and effort, and I smiled back at him. "We have to go to Target so I can walk and jumpstart this labor, because today is the day! I am going to have this baby today!" I am sure he was sorry he had bothered to ask.

Within a couple hours we were strolling down the aisles of a local Target store. I am still not exactly sure why I chose Target instead of Walmart or the mall. Perhaps I vaguely remembered our previous mad-dash to Walmart while in the throes of labor with my first pregnancy (you can read about that in chapter ten). Whatever the reason, the walking was well underway.

While we walked the halls of Target, we saw the Principal of our oldest daughter's School. "What are you all doing here?" she asked.

Tony diverted his eyes while I triumphantly declared, "Today is the day. We are going to have the baby today." She congratulated us and I continued on my mission.

After an hour or so, I recognized that I was feeling more hunger pains than labor pains and we headed for lunch. My husband was a trooper and supported me through the entire escapade. The day passed uneventfully and soon early evening had arrived. Throughout the day I went through spurts of contractions, but they did not maintain consistency needed to indicate full blown labor.

I was thirty-seven or so weeks pregnant, not quite forty, but I was tired and I was ready. I am a registered nurse and I know well that thirty-seven weeks could be too early for many people to go into labor. I know well the potential dangers of going into labor before the baby is fully developed and ready to be born. Yet, I knew that it was time for this baby to come forth. My first daughter was also born at thirty-seven weeks, (though that labor happened completely spontaneously). Anyway, I just knew that the long-awaited time had arrived.

From the beginning of the pregnancy until the end I experienced nausea and insomnia. I was desperate for a good night's sleep. My midwife eventually recommended something for me to take occasionally due to the extreme

Standing on the Promises

insomnia. Don't get me wrong, I loved being pregnant. I fully recognized it as one of God's most precious gifts to us and the opportunity to bring forth another life is a blessing beyond words. Nevertheless, my body was screaming for deliverance from the thirty-seven weeks of pain, sickness, soreness, insomnia and a daily worsening sciatic nerve condition. Toward the end of my pregnancy it was determined that the baby was nicely positioned directly on my sciatic nerve. This made walking, sitting, standing and even lying down almost unbearable at times. I was tired, exhausted, sleep deprived, overwhelmed and in pain. I was at my wit's end and knew that the season for this baby to come forth had finally arrived.

At times the journey towards reaching you promise may be trying or even unpleasant. Just like the span of a pregnancy, there is a span of preparation that precedes the birthing of many plans, dreams and promises. To be said simply, it takes work! Bringing forth your hopes and dreams usually will not happen unless there is some sort of effort on your part. Just hoping and desiring something to come forth is not enough. Even standing in faith must be accompanied with corresponding action! The Bible says it best, "faith without works is dead." On the road to birthing your promise, you must not lose heart. Continue to set goals and take deliberate action toward reaching your hopes and dreams. It would seem silly for someone to desire having a baby, but then take no steps toward making that desire happen. Likewise, you may have a goal or dream. Do not sit around and wait for it to supernaturally appear. Look to God for direction, develop your strategy and plan of action, and persevere! The road to birthing your promise may not be an easy road, but it can be accomplished. When the pains of life arise in your life, do not give up. Keep pressing, keep hoping and keep working! "In the same way, faith by itself, if it is not accompanied by action, is dead," (James 2:17 NIV).

When you know it is time, you will not give up. I was not hoping that today was the day, I knew it. At five p.m. when my attempts at jump starting labor still had not succeeded, a new determination arose within me. I knew in my heart that today was the day and I would not be denied. The contractions were coming and had been for some days, but they were not quite consistent enough. I laced up my athletic shoes and walked outside with my big thirty-seven week belly.

"Where are you going honey?" my husband yelled.

"Get ready," I shouted back. "It's almost time to go to the hospital." I didn't wait for his response. I was determined. I knew that something was about to come forth that day and I was filled with expectation and anticipation. I walked across our front yard to the sidewalk in front of our house. I started walking up and down the fairly steep hill that stretched the span of our block. I am sure I was a hilarious sight with my bright green running suit and large pregnant belly. I didn't care what anyone thought. My time had arrived and I was moving with sheer determination. I walked up the hill and down the hill, up the hill and down the hill. I could feel the contractions begin to intensify. They were coming quicker now. Sheer determination burned in my eyes and spurred me onward.

My husband watched curiously from the front yard. After two hours, the contraction were intense and consistently every three to five minutes. I walked up to my husband and said with a smile the words I had been waiting for months to say "get the car, it's time."

Tony looked at me in utter amazement. "It's time?" he asked.

"Yes!" I shouted. "It is time. Get the car!"

Tony helped me into the car and we headed for the hospital. We arrived in maternity triage that night around eight p.m. and by ten p.m. they had admitted me to a room. I was in full blown labor. I spent the next several hours walking the hospital hallways with my husband tagging along. I had been walking off and on that day and now through the night. The most amazing thing to me was the absence of pain. I had been praying for labor to be supernatural in every way, and fellow friends and intercessors from our church were praying for us as well. By the time I dilated to four cm with no pain at all I began to wonder what was going on. Sure, we had prayed for a supernatural delivery, but where was the pain?

The delivery of my first child was nothing short of sheer agony. With my first delivery, I was in so much excruciating pain that I drifted in and out of consciousness at the check-in area! I was a wreck! I was wheeled to a room and given some medication within minutes of arrival, because I started losing consciousness due to the pain. So, you can imagine my surprise that this second labor was progressing without any pain..

Whatever You Do, Don't Sneeze!

I dilated to four cm and still no pain. I wondered what was going on. This was a far cry from the agony of my first labor. I know we had been praying for a supernatural labor but this was unbelievable. Sure I am a Christian, but a labor with no pain, this challenged my faith as well as everything I had been taught as a nurse. Later that night the midwife came in and broke my water. Even that only caused mild discomfort. For the next several hours, my labor stalled at five cm. I walked and swayed but still no progress. I became discouraged.

At times the process of bringing forth your hopes and dreams may stall. You can be moving along at a great place and suddenly, things seem to slow down or stop completely. Do not lose heart. Ward off discouragement and remain focused. Keep working towards bring forth your dreams.

The midwife shared that they would like to give me some pitocin to help speed up labor and strengthen the contractions. They did so and asked if I wanted to get an epidural. I was familiar with pitocin and knew that it can intensify contractions significantly, which can also bring on the pain. I was on the fence. My last experience with childbirth was horribly unimaginable, but so far this labor had been totally pain-free, a supernatural experience. I was halfway to ten cm, but fear started to creep in. Should we go for the total supernatural labor or get the epidural just in case the pain kicked in later? After remembering the pain of my first labor, I erred on the side of caution, and opted for the epidural.

Post-epidural, I settled down in the hospital bed to get some well needed sleep, and the beginnings of regret tugged at my heart. Had I failed my test? Did my faith fail when it should have stood? God had already moved in a miraculous way over the past twenty-four hours, letting me know that it was time for the baby to come forth, and then giving me a great labor without pain. Yet, fear kept me from totally trusting God and believing that He would see me through the entirety supernaturally. I drifted off into a restful sleep hoping and praying that I had not missed my opportunity for a supernatural delivery. I took comfort in knowing that my promise was well on the way and would soon be in my arms, sooner than I realized.

Around eight a.m. my nurse came in. I was feeling great as most post-epidural recipients do. I shared with the nurse that I was started to feel something down below.

"Pressure, or an urge to push?" she asked hopefully.

"Yes, something like that." I answered.

The nurse took a look and yelled for my midwife to come right away.

"Christina!" she exclaimed staring me in the eye. "Whatever you do, don't sneeze!"

Now that's a strange thing to tell a woman in labor. I assure you I will never forget those words. To our amazement, precious Gabrielle was about to make her entrance into the world. She could not wait any longer. She was ready to come forth. One small push and a few moments later, I was holding Gabby in my arms. I ended up having a powerfully supernatural labor and delivery after all. Gabby was born with one tiny push and no pain, weighing in at a healthy seven pounds and three ounces. God answered our prayers in a mighty way.

The Anguish of Waiting

At times a season of waiting can span months or even years. Abraham was ninety-nine years when he and Sarah conceived Isaac. Joseph received a dream from God revealing his forthcoming destiny and promotion, yet a span of at least thirteen years passed before he entered into the full manifestation of this promise. We have to realize that God's timing is not our own, and His ways and timing far exceed our finite minds and understanding. His ways are perfect and often times beyond our reasoning and comprehension.

The story of Hannah was shared in chapter 11 of this book. Hannah had faith, and knew that if she persevered and kept returning to the presence of the Lord, then something had to change. Yes, she was barren, but there was a promise on the inside of her that she refused to let die. There was a hope within her that kept her from sleeping at night. Her faith just would not allow her to give up on what God had promised her. Hannah understood that if she could just get into the presence of the Lord, a change would occur in her circumstance. She would conceive and the dead places down on the inside of her had to wake-up. Likewise, there may be some dead or barren places in your own life, family, marriage, finances and relationships. Areas that are not producing and it may seem like all hope is lost. Know that God specializes in miracles and with Him nothing is impossible. Just as He released life to Hannah's womb and caused her to conceive and bring forth, after a lifetime of barrenness and disappointments, so can it be with you. Continue to worship the Lord and bring your requests to Him as Hannah did. Refuse to let disappointment and discouragement steal your hope and joy. The promises of God are sure, and if He spoke or released a promise concerning your life, you must continue to believe and trust in that promise. Refuse to be denied.

In seasons of waiting the key is do not give up. It is much easier to give up on your promise than to stand in faith until it fully manifests. Everything in life will not come easily. There are times when you must persevere against all odds and wait on God to release what He has promised you. Frustration frequents this place, especially when you attempt to confine God to your timetable and deadlines. His ways are far greater than yours and as it is often said, His timing is always perfect.

What is it that you have been called to bring forth in the earth? What is it? You cannot allow your dreams to die, even if you face stiff opposition as Hannah did. Hannah refused to give up on her promise. I encourage you to have that same stance. Eventually, Hannah stopped fighting the winds of her storm and she allowed those winds to push her forward right into her destiny. Do not allow opposition to slow you down; instead let it ignite a new determination within you. A determination to do and accomplish what you know God has placed in your heart.

Epilogue

You are not the sum total of your past experiences! You are so much more than that. You are who God created you to be, and every promise that God has for your life is still active and closer than you think. I shared in the Introduction of this book that I felt downright foolish when I walked away from a great paying job and job security, after a dream in the night, to follow God's leading. I felt downright foolish. Few people were able to understand why I did what I did. I received much criticism that was difficult to endure. However, along my journey I discovered that God uses the foolish things to confound the wise. Once I stopped worrying about what everyone else was thinking and saying about me, my purpose and destiny came into clearer view. Did I ever imagine that I would be a preacher, teacher, conference speaker and published author? Never in a million years. I didn't see this coming, but once the Lord started to reveal my path, a desire was birthed in my heart. My road to unshakable faith started out as a road filled with fear and doubt, but as I progressed and took a stand upon the Word and promises of God, fear was exchanged for unshakable faith!

Remember, unshakable faith is the willingness to believe and not move from that place of believing, no matter what is transpiring around you. Unshakable faith means that you believe in something, even when no one else believes in it, and you refuse to be shaken by their inability to see it. Unshakable faith refuses to be shaken by the storms of life. Unshakable faith is just that, unshakable!

Beloved, I encourage you to not give up! Do not allow your faith to become weary. Every hope, dream, vision and goal you have been carrying in your heart is yours to apprehend. Do not allow anyone to kill your dreams or diminish your faith. Take deliberate steps in the direction of your purpose and destiny. Let faith fuel every step that you take!

Refuse to be stopped by rejection, failure and disappointments. What God promised you is yours, but you must keep believing and working towards those goals. Refuse to be denied! Let your faith soar. You may make some wrong turns along the way, but that is no reason to give up. When you experience denial, setbacks and rejection, do not give up. Keep believing and pressing forward. The "yes" you have been waiting on could be the next answer you receive. Do not give up prematurely.

Your dreams were not intended to stay in the realm of dreams. At some point you must transition from dreaming, to believing, to pursuing to fulfilling! The road of unshakable faith is before you. This road may seem foolish. It may stretch your faith farther than it has been stretched before. The road of unshakable faith is a destiny road and it is yours for the taking. Plant your feet firmly on the promises of God, and go forward with soaring faith, into all that you have been called to do and fulfill in the earth.

Make every day count.

Anything is possible to those who believe…

Notes

Chapter 6

1. Strong, James, L.L.D.,S.T.D., John Kohlenberg III, and James A. Swanson. *The Strongest Strong's Exhaustive Concordance of the Bible.* Grand Rapids: Zondervan, 2001. For further information on meaning of Greek word histemi, see 2476 (p. 1617).

Chapter 9

1. Strong, James, L.L.D.,S.T.D., John Kohlenberg III, and James A. Swanson. *The Strongest Strong's Exhaustive Concordance of the Bible.* Grand Rapids: Zondervan, 2001. For further information on meaning of Hebrew word hapes or chaphets, see 2654 (p. 1502).

Scripture references marked NKJV are taken from the New King James Version. Copyright 1979, 1980, 1982, Thomas Nelson, Inc.

Scripture references marked KJV are taken from the King James Version of the Bible.

About the Author

CHRISTINA M. WHITAKER is a nurse who worked for fifteen years in the psychiatric field. She is a licensed minister and director of prayer and prophetic ministries at World Victory International Christian Center. Whitaker believes in the power of prayer and desires to see all experience healing and success in their lives. She speaks at conferences, trainings and workshops throughout the United States. She is married to Antonio Whitaker. They reside in North Carolina with their two daughters.